Coolidge and the Historians

Studies in Statesmanship
Harry V. Jaffa, Winston S. Churchill Association,
General Editor

Coolidge and the Historians

Thomas B. Silver

Carolina Academic Press
for The Claremont Institute

Durham, North Carolina

To my father and mother

Library of Congress Catalog Card Number: 82-73242
International Standard Book Number: 0-89089-037-4 (cloth)
0-89089-038-2 (paper)

Second Printing
Printed in the United States of America

Carolina Academic Press
Post Office Box 8795
Durham, North Carolina 27707

Contents

Foreword

July 4, 1982: The 110th Anniversary of Calvin Coolidge's Birth

When President Reagan entered the White House, he rearranged the portraits in the Cabinet Room, replacing Thomas Jefferson's with Calvin Coolidge's. I think Calvin Coolidge would have been more honored if his portrait had been side by side with that of the author of the Declaration of Independence. Coolidge is the only President of the United States to have been born on the Fourth of July. This is something seldom remembered, and one wonders whether President Reagan remembered it. Abraham Lincoln once remarked that "The principles of Jefferson are the definitions and axioms of free society." And, in a speech delivered in Independence Hall, in February of 1861, on his way to his inauguration as sixteenth President of the United States, Lincoln said "that all the political sentiments I entertain have been drawn . . . from the sentiments which originated and were given to the world from this hall. I have never had a feeling politically that did not spring from the sentiments embodied in the Declaration of Independence." Calvin Coolidge might have said the same thing, as he is the most notable interpreter of the Declaration since Abraham Lincoln.

There are few today who think of Coolidge, when they consider the tradition that was founded upon July 4, 1776. For this, our national life and national purpose suffer greatly, because that life and that purpose have no vitality and no guidance that do not spring from that source. Mr. Reagan remembers the Coolidge years—from 1923 until 1929—because they were years of uncommon prosperity, peace, and optimism. They were years preceded by war and depression, and they were years followed by depression and war. Mr. Reagan thinks that the magic of those golden years was due in no small measure to the wisdom and dignity with which Calvin Coolidge conducted the office of the President of the United States. He does so, however, in the teeth of the conventional wisdom of the historical establishment, which looks upon the Coolidge boom merely as the prelude to a bust, and who thinks of the optimism of those years as a fool's paradise. The "Puritan in Babylon," according to such *cognoscenti* as Arthur Schlesinger, Jr., heard no evil, saw no evil, and spoke no evil, and thereby let the nation stumble into disaster.

July 4, 1982, marks the one hundred and tenth anniversary of Calvin Coolidge's birth. Happily, this year will also mark the publication of Thomas B. Silver's *Coolidge and the Historians*. This will, we trust, mark as well the beginning of a new era in the appreciation, by scholars and publicists, of the life and public services of Calvin Coolidge. Never, we think, has a received opinion been more ruthlessly and relentlessly challenged and demolished, than has the currently orthodox historical judgment of Calvin Coolidge, in the pages of *Coolidge and the Historians*. Mr. Silver has given us an intellectual *tour de force* in his demonstration of how, in Winston Churchill's phrase, two generations of historians "have followed each other, like sheep, through the gates of error." Mr. Silver's book, at the minimum, substantiates President Reagan's memory of the 1920's, as a more accurate guide to the political reality of those years, than anything written by the court historians of the New Deal and of the New Frontier.

Any final judgment concerning Calvin Coolidge's presidency must await a fresh scholarly assessment. Until now, there simply has been no sufficient research in depth on these years. But there is no doubt that in Coolidge's many occasional writings and speeches on the American political tradition, we find statesmanship in one of its highest manifestations. More than Theodore or Franklin Roosevelt, more than Woodrow Wilson, Coolidge saw high office as "preeminently a place of moral leadership." In "Great Virginians," he wrote,

> We meet here out of reverence for the past. We come with that resolution, which has characterized Americans, to show by our actions our adherence to those seasoned and established principles which have made our country the greatest among the nations of the earth.

Later, in the same speech, he continued,

> It is only when men begin to worship that they begin to grow. A wholesome regard for the memory of the great men of long ago is the best assurance to a people of a continuation of great men to come, who shall be able to instruct, to lead, and to inspire. A people who worship at the shrine of true greatness will themselves be truly great.

Calvin Coolidge's first notable achievement as a young man was when, as a senior at Amherst, he entered a contest sponsored by the Sons of the American Revolution. This contest was for the best essay on the causes of the American Revolution. The gold medal, for first prize, in 1895, was awarded to Calvin Coolidge of Amherst. For all his reserve, Coolidge was proud enough of this essay to reprint it in *The Price of Freedom*, a collection of his speeches and addresses, published by Scribner's, in March of 1924, during the first year of his presidency. Few under-

graduate essays, whether at Amherst or elsewhere, could
have stood the test of publication, after thirty years. In it,
we see the beginning of a life-long devotion to the articulation and understanding of "those seasoned and established
principles which have made our country the greatest among
the nations of the earth." And we see at the core of Coolidge's political being, a life-long devotion to the memory
of the men and events, by which these principles were
enshrined in our institutions of law and of constitutional
government. Abraham Lincoln, in hs speech on "The Per-
petuation of our Political Institutions," delivered before
the Young Men's Lyceum of Springfield, Illinois, January
27, 1838, sounded what was to become the central theme
of his own career: how the political order in the service of
civil and religious liberty, might come to be regarded as
sacred, even within the sphere of secular government. For
Lincoln did not think the Constitution, or the rule of law,
could survive the challenge of the unruly human passions,
unless it was invested with the same kind of sanctity as "the
only greater institution." That, of course, was the underly-
ing premise both of the Gettysburg Address and of the
Second Inaugural. This Lincolnian premise underlay as
well a large body of Coolidge's occasional speeches and
essays. His preoccupation with the American political tradition, and his conception of political leadership as instruc-
tion in that tradition, invest the rule of law with the respect
that is ordinarily reserved for the symbols and events of
revealed religion. A mere listing of some of the titles in *The
Price of Freedom* will suggest this. Among them are "The
Pilgrims," "The Power of Moral Law," "Theodore Roosevelt," "The Title of America," "Our Heritage from Hamil-
ton," "The Place of Lincoln," "Ulysses S. Grant," "Great
Virginians," "The Old North Church," "The Destiny of
America," "The Green Mountains." These are no mere
collections of pious and patriotic cliches. They are deeply

informed by historical learning. The essays on notable men
are surprisingly reminiscent of the characterological insight
of Churchill's *Great Contemporaries*. They are certainly in
harmony with Churchill's conviction that human destiny is
largely the result of human character, and that whatever
the role of chance, history in its decisive moments reflects
human wisdom and human folly. Coolidge had no more
patience than Churchill with that "brainy sort of people"
who would divest mankind of moral responsibility, by telling us that we are creatures of society, or of history, or of
buried motives that are beyond our ken. Coolidge's address
on Theodore Roosevelt begins with words that might have
introduced many others as well. It is a typical Coolidge
sentence, and it is redolent of the liberal education in
which he was steeped. "Great men are the ambassadors of
Providence sent to reveal to their fellow men their unknown
selves."

We regard it then as an act of Providence, that the child,
born on the Fourth of July, 1872, whose prize essay on the
causes of the American Revolution, in 1895, first brought
him distinction, should have been President of the United
States in 1926, when the nation observed its one hundred
and fiftieth anniversary. It is a badge of our shame that, in
1976, no one in authority seems to have noted what Calvin
Coolidge had said half a century earlier. This is all the more
regrettable, when one contemplates the intellectual pov-
erty of the speeches and addresses of our two hundredth
anniversary. The center of the nation's attention was absorbed
in the televised sailing of the tall ships into New York
Harbor. However beautiful was this reminder of the age of
sail, no one doubted that that age had been superseded
forever. If the Declaration of Independence was remembered at all, it was with a nostalgic fondness, as if it too had
been a tall ship.

Coolidge's speech in Independence Hall, July 5, 1926,

was entitled "The Inspiration of the Declaration of Independence." It was a profound exploration of the historical and philosophical meaning of that famous document. Coolidge never doubted for a moment that the importance of American independence was to be found in the principles by which that independence was originally justified. They were principles which—however beautiful—could never be superseded. "It was not because it was proposed to establish a new nation, but because it was proposed to establish a nation on new principles, that July 4, 1776, has come to be regarded as one of the greatest days in history." The truths expressed in the Declaration, he said, were very old. But never before had they been adopted by a duly authorized and constituted representative body, a body supported by general public opinion, and by armies in the field. It was this uniting of philosophical thought with political action that made the Declaration of Independence "the most important civil document in the world."

Near the end of his oration, Coolidge remarked that there was, about the Declaration, "a finality that is exceedingly restful." The assertions of man's equality, of his endowment with inalienable rights, of the derivation of the just powers of government from the consent of the governed are all, he insisted, final. "No advance, no progress can be beyond these propositions." Anyone wishing to deny them, he went on, can only go backward. And those who wish to proceed in such a direction "are reactionary." Coolidge spoke in the heyday of the so-called "Progressive Era." The idea that a final political truth might be pronounced at any time was wholly inconsistent with the evolutionary, historicist, and relativist theories that dominated his world—as they still dominate our own. Much of the unfavorable writing about Coolidge has stemmed from inability of the writers to take seriously anyone who himself took seriously such a classical idea of truth, as a final cause of moral and political action. But Coolidge was wiser than his critics, and wiser than the fashionable "intellectuals" of the academy and of the media, of his day and of ours.

Although at the time of the sesqui-centennial, Coolidge spoke in the midst of unprecedented prosperity, he reminded his countrymen that the cause of that prosperity was more important than the prosperity itself. "On an occasion like this a great temptation exists to present evidence of the practical success of our form of government . . . But it is not results and effects so much as sources and causes that . . . it is . . . necessary to contemplate."

> We live in an age of science and of abounding accumulation of material things. These did not create our Declaration. Our Declaration created them. The things of the spirit come first. Unless we cling to that, all of our prosperity, overwhelming though it may appear, will turn to a barren sceptre in our grasp.
> If we are to maintain the great heritage which has been bequeathed to us, we must be likeminded as the fathers who created it. We must cultivate the reverence which they had for the things that are holy.

Let us hope that, as Ronald Reagan—and his successors in the White House—glance from time to time at the portrait of our scholarly and philosophical and poetic twenty-ninth President, they may in his spirit draw increased devotion to that great heritage which it is their highest duty to transmit unimpaired.

Harry V. Jaffa
President, Winston S. Churchill Association
Claremont, California
July 4, 1982

Acknowledgments

That person will be mistaken who believes that this book was prompted by recent political developments. It is, in fact, a revised version of a doctoral dissertation, which was completed in the spring of 1980.

I wish to thank several people who have helped in the preparation of the book. Peter Schramm and Christopher Flannery, all too many years ago, read the germinal essay of my dissertation (Chapter I) and criticized it thoroughly. As a result, it was substantially revised. Their criticisms helped to set the tone and direction of subsequent chapters.

Professor Harry V. Jaffa, chairman of my dissertation committee at the Claremont Graduate School, reviewed my work as it progressed. His constant encouragement sharpened my focus and my will, even if it did not quicken my pace.

Professors George Blair and William B. Allen served as readers on my dissertation committee. I have benefitted from their telling comments.

During the writing of the dissertation I was assisted by fellowships from the Earhart Foundation of Ann Arbor, Michigan and the Intercollegiate Studies Institute of Bryn Mawr, Pennsylvania. A grant from The Henry Salvatori Center at Claremont McKenna College permitted me to take some time off to prepare the dissertation for publication. Dr. George C. S. Benson, director of the Salvatori

Center, was good enough to read the entire manuscript and to make a number of suggestions that I have followed, especially in rewriting the final chapter.

Eldon Alexander, Mickey Craig, and William Flannery compiled the index.

In the end, L. P. Arnn went over the complete text. He made numerous corrections and suggestions, both of substance and of usage.

I have alluded to the fact that this book was written at a pace that would have made even Calvin Coolidge restless and fidgety. In the meantime my wife and son looked on, like two stoics, as the work progressed. In his *Autobiography* Calvin Coolidge said of his wife: "For almost a quarter of a century she has borne with my infirmities, and I have rejoiced in her graces." The only reason that I cannot say exactly the same is that I haven't yet known my wife for a quarter of a century.

Introduction

Think back upon a decade of upheaval in American history. The country's youngest president, having succeeded a conservative Republican and having sounded a clarion call to the progressive forces in the country, is now gone forever from the presidency. An activist Democratic president skillfully shepherds legislation through Congress, but wolfish war follows close upon the heels of domestic reform. Radical protests against the system, and a few bombings, ignite national hysteria. The president retires in bitterness, soon to die. His Republican successor at first holds forth the hope of restoring the national composure; but he is replaced by his vice-president after a truncated term marred by economic dislocation and executive scandal unprecedented in American history.

Would it pass understanding if the new president set aside his clarion so that he might speak softly to his countrymen? As there are times during the nation's history that require its citizens to summon up their last reserves of daring and courage, are there not other times that call for the exercise of moderation and sobriety? Does not Prudence comprehend all of the virtues?

Imagine a statesman ascending to the presidency after a decade of war, national hysteria, recession, and scandal. Imagine that the next five years are characterized by peace, national calm, unprecedented, inflation-free prosperity, and rigid executive integrity. Would not the citizens bestow their gratitude upon the statesman who presided over such a time? And if it is true, as a famous political scientist once said, that we approach the subject of prudence by studying those to whom we attribute it, would not such a statesman perhaps be worthy of the attention of our political scientists and political historians?

But prudence, of course, is no longer among the guiding themes of political thought. Nowadays many if not most political scientists disparage any president who does not plunge headlong into the future, stung by the whip and the spur of ideological impatience. The very idea of the imperial presidency was not, in its original version, detachable from the ideology of progress. The political scientists who invented the new science of politics at the dawn of the twentieth century understood the imperial presidency to be an ingredient in that blend of ideological daring and political power which would conquer, once and for all, the natural rhythm of crisis and calm, ebb and flow, in political affairs. Continuous progress would result from consciously directed, continuous revolution, and politics would be progressively freed from tragedy and sorrow.

From time to time, of course, disillusionment with this or that president causes people to wonder whether that blend of daring and power is a scientific prescription or an alchemist's brew. But most of us have been satisfied to criticize the excesses of daring rather than to question daring itself. Daring itself has always been excused by the inertia of the American political system, an inertia that is said to be congenial to an unholy alliance of self-interested and ideological opponents of change. But daring is only a necessary condition for overcoming this inertia. Daring must be joined to power: A great body at rest will be moved only by a great force directed upon it.

When we spoke at the outset of this introduction about a decade of upheaval in American history, we had in mind the period from the first administration of Woodrow Wilson to the death of President Harding. During the five years following the decade 1914 to 1923, President Calvin Coolidge won the admiration and the gratitude of the American people. His three predecessors had begun their terms full of hope for the future, and had ended them, respectively, in defeat, repudiation, and death. Coolidge inherited the leadership of his party and his country near a trough in their fortunes, and by the day of his retirement had brought them to a crest which neither would see again for a generation. The hallmarks of the years preceding Coolidge were war and depression; the hallmarks of the years following were depression and war. The hallmarks of the Coolidge era were prosperity and peace.

President Coolidge has not, however, won the admiration and gratitude of our political scientists and political historians. "The fact is that no historians write favorably about the twelve-year Republican interregnum compared with the Progressive Era that preceded it and the New Deal that followed."[1] This statement is hardly less true today than it was when Basil Rauch wrote it twenty years ago. In 1962 Professor Arthur Schlesinger, Sr. published the results of a poll in which seventy-five American historians ranked thirty-one of the presidents. The average rank of the three Republican presidents of the twenties was twenty-sixth out of thirty-one. The average rank of their immediate predecessor and their two New Deal successors (who coincidentally were the first three Democratic presidents of the twentieth century) was fifth out of thirty-one.

Most historians write briefly about the thirtieth president, and they reach similar conclusions expressed in similar words. A standard account of Calvin Coolidge and the politics of the roaring twenties may be found in *A*

1. Basil Rauch, "Roosevelt and the Historians," *Yale Review*, June 1957, p. 615.

Pocket History of the United States by Allan Nevins and
Henry Steele Commager. This book, written by two of
America's most distinguished historians, has gone through
six editions and has sold more than two million copies.

Nevins and Commager state that Presidents Harding
and Coolidge pursued a dual policy of laissez-faire capitalism and government subsidies to private enterprise. Whether
one or the other approach was used in a particular case
depended upon whether or not it would help business.

> In the domestic arena, the Harding administration inaugurated
> the reign of "normalcy"—and Harding's idea of normalcy
> was a return to the good old days of Mark Hanna and
> McKinley. This was not, as is sometimes supposed, pure
> laissez-faire, but rather a felicitous combination of two
> policies—one, freedom of private enterprise from
> governmental restraint, and the other, generous subsidies to
> private enterprise. Government withdrew from business, but
> business moved in and shaped most government policies.[2]

The obverse of concern for business was indifference
toward other groups in society, especially disadvantaged
groups.

> . . . concern for equality of opportunity would have come with
> better grace had the Harding and Coolidge administrations
> shown a sincere and sustained interest in the welfare of labor
> and farmer groups. But these administrations were
> interested only in the "businessman," and their conception
> of business was a narrow one. Neither the farmers nor the
> workingman shared the piping prosperity of the twenties.
> There was a brief but short break in farm prices in 1921; by
> the mid-twenties a gradual decline set in and continued
> without interruption until the operation of the New Deal
> reforms became effective . . .

2. Henry Steele Commager and Allan Nevins, *A Pocket History of the United States*, 6th ed. (New York: Pocket Books, 1976), pp. 405-406.

> Yet in the face of this situation the Harding and Coolidge
> administrations, so eager to place the government at the
> disposal of business, evinced an attitude of indifference to
> the farming interests.[3]

Calvin Coolidge, seen through the eyes of most historians, is no more agreeable in his person than he is in his
policies. Nevins and Commager deride him as "a thoroughly limited politician, dour and unimaginative, thrifty
of words and ideas, devoted to the maintenance of the
status quo, and morbidly suspicious of liberalism in any
form."[4]

A similar portrait of Coolidge may be found in *The
Oxford History of the American People*, by Samuel Eliot
Morison. This book is one of the most popular contemporary surveys of American history. In July of 1965, after its
first eleven weeks on the best seller list, the *Oxford History* had already sold sixty thousand copies in hardback. Two
hundred fifty thousand more were printed for the Book-
of-the-Month Club, and the book has since been widely
read in paperback as well. Morison had a reputation (and
deservedly so) as one of the finest historians of this century.

What did all of those readers learn from Morison about
Calvin Coolidge? If they made it to page 933 of the *Oxford
History*, they learned that Coolidge, the second of the
three "inept" Republican presidents of the twenties, was
mean, thin-lipped, little, mediocre, parsimonious, not as
bright as people thought, dour, unimaginative, abstemious,
frugal, unpretentious, taciturn, an admirer of wealthy men,
reactionary, a cynical doubter of the progressive movement, and democratic only by habit not by conviction. As
president, Coolidge exalted inactivity. He took it easy in
the White House with a long nap every afternoon. He

3. Ibid., pp. 407-408.
4. Ibid., p. 408.

maintained his feeble health by riding on a mechanical horse.

On the plus side, Coolidge had a moral integrity that was lacking in Harding.[5]

The *Oxford History,* as it happens, ends with a description of another president from Massachusetts, John F. Kennedy.

> President Kennedy was remarkable not only for his courage
> and wisdom in meeting the challenges of our day; he chose to
> take the most important steps ever made by a President of
> the United States to foster literature and the arts. . . . He did
> his best to impart to the public his respect for excellence
> and dislike of mediocrity . . .

He and Jackie "were the first presidential couple within the memory of White House gardeners to care about the flower gardens." They surrounded themselves with "gay, active, intelligent people . . ." "At the same time they were an image of the typical American family, frolicking with their children and taking pleasure trips to the country . . ." *"Everything that the Kennedy's did* was done with grace, elegance, and style, and it all seemed natural, not forced . . ."

> . . . the memory of that bright, vivid personality, that great
> gentleman *whose every act and appearance* appealed to our
> pride and gave us fresh pride in ourselves and our country,
> will live in us for a long, long time. (Italics mine.)

The *Oxford History* ends with the score of Camelot: "Ask every person if he's heard the story; and tell it strong and clear if he has not: That once there was a fleeting wisp of glory—called Camelot."[6]

5. Samuel Eliot Morison, *The Oxford History of the American People* (New
   York: Oxford University Press, 1965), pp. 933-934.
6. Ibid., pp. 1120-1122.

Everyone knows that political debate is often a species of caricature. Politicians in the heat of battle tend to be fastidiously accurate neither in their portrayal of their opponents nor in their portrayal of themselves. Generally speaking, in a democracy the best political strategy is to persuade the electorate that you stand somewhere near the middle of the bell-shaped curve and that your opponent occupies one of the extremes. The high duty of the historian, on the other hand, is to eschew caricature in the name of truth. He wishes to see, and to present, things as they are. This is particularly difficult in the writing of recent history because the historian's own political passions are likely to be engaged. The conscientious historian, therefore, takes special care to draw his heroes and villains true to life. Such care is perhaps more evident in our own times than it was formerly, given the professionalization of history. In the writing of history, writes Professor Arthur Schlesinger Jr.,

> Our taste today is more fastidious, our canons of scholarship more rigorous, our partialities more contained, our diagnosis more complex, our judgment more tolerant.[7]

When it comes to Calvin Coolidge, though, one wonders whether the professor's description of contemporary historiography holds true. Coolidge has been subjected to more ridicule perhaps than any other president in American history. His policies are regarded by most historians as beneath contempt. The passages quoted above from Nevins, Commager, and Morison are, in our opinion, far from objective.

By objective we do not mean value-free. We do not assert that historians should be neutral toward men and policies. On the contrary, the duty of the historian, like

7. Arthur Schlesinger, "The Historian as Artist," *Atlantic*, July 1963, p. 40.

that of the politician or the citizen, is to take sides. But the historian is in a more fortunate situation than is the politician. The historian is not caught in the rush and uncertainty of great events; he is not compelled to strive for immediate political victories or advantages; he is free of the successful politician's necessary deference to the opinions of his constituents. The historian is to the politician much as the judge is to the lawyer. They both take sides, but the lawyer takes one side from the outset and strives with all his might to make it prevail, while the judge takes sides only after giving a fair and full hearing to all parties involved. It is our view that Calvin Coolidge has not had such a hearing from our leading historians.

Our intention in the essays that follow is to review the career of Calvin Coolidge during its final ten years. In so doing we hope to re-open certain questions that most history books treat as closed. Throughout this review we will frequently use as our foil a very influential history of the 1920s, *The Crisis of the Old Order*, by Professor Arthur M. Schlesinger, Jr. ("The importance of Schlesinger's *Age of Roosevelt* is that it promises to do more than any other book so far published to win the struggle for interpretation of our modern history in favor of reformism . . .").[8]

In Chapter 1 we will look at Calvin Coolidge the man through the eyes of Professor Schlesinger. As we do so we will try to harken back to the professor's own words on the writing of history. Fastidiousness, rigor, impartiality, complexity, and tolerance: Let these be our touchstones as we explore the past.

8. Rauch, "Roosevelt," p. 618.

One

Calvin Coolidge

Perhaps the most memorable historical sketch of Calvin Coolidge is to be found in *The Crisis of the Old Order*,[1] the first volume in Professor Schlesinger's *Age of Roosevelt*. Coolidge is interesting to Professor Schlesinger, we believe, less in himself than as a symbol of American conservatism more generally. Schlesinger understands twentieth century American conservatism as rigid ideological opposition to the moderate and pragmatic tradition of liberal reform in America.

According to Schlesinger, such progress as is possible in a democracy is smoothest when it issues from a creative tension between a right and a left whose tempers are empirical rather than ideological, whose goals and expectations are moderate, and whose love of the common good is strong. But the story of American conservatism, he believes, has too often been the story of rigid, ideologically motivated opposition to change. American conservatism is a dam without sluices thrown across the river of history. Moreover, the conservative ideology reflects the mentality of a class, the possessing class in America. Schlesinger deplores the acquisitive character of American conservatism and its tendency to promote the interests of businessmen and the rich at the expense of the common good.

These two themes—the curse of ideology and the curse

---

1. Arthur M. Schlesinger, Jr., *The Crisis of the Old Order* (Boston: Houghton Mifflin Company, 1957), p. 5.

of acquisitiveness—are vividly personified in *The Crisis of the Old Order* in the characterizations of Herbert Hoover and Calvin Coolidge, the spokesmen for an idea whose time had gone. In Schlesinger's view, Hoover was a tragic figure in American conservatism and Coolidge a comic one. Hoover was, or became, an ideologue, who did not sufficiently understand that all ideas must be scrutinized regularly to see whether they have outlived their usefulness. Progress in politics—to the extent that it is possible —depends upon the shattering of complacency. If we make it our business to challenge our own complacency unceasingly, then we shall perhaps avoid the trauma of having events challenge it for us. This was the trauma and the tragedy of Herbert Hoover, a man of high ideals, flawed by his self-righteousness and cast down by events. The tragic figure of Hoover contrasts with the comic figure of Calvin Coolidge, the smugly self-righteous little man of low ideals. Coolidge transformed the dollar into the Almighty Dollar and worshipped unceasingly at its altar.

Professor Schlesinger's thematic discussion of the political thought and the personality of Calvin Coolidge covers about three pages of *The Crisis of the Old Order*.[2] This section follows a quotation from Dwight Morrow in which Coolidge is described as the man of character America needed in the oily wake of Teapot Dome. Schlesinger is interested, in the face of that claim, to see what kind of man Coolidge was. He adduces the testimony of three witnesses (aside from a brief remark by the British Ambassador) to show us what Coolidge was like. The first is Arthur Vandenberg, who tells us that Coolidge was "unimpressive" as vice-president. The second is William Allen White, whose testimony is taken from a letter in which White compares Coolidge to Old Scrooge. The final wit-

2. Ibid., pp. 56-58.

ness is Ike Hoover, the White House usher, who tells all about Coolidge's odd and distasteful personal habits. One might wish that our historian had canvassed a somewhat wider sample of Coolidge's contemporaries; but we must work with what we have been given.

Professor Schlesinger begins his depiction of Coolidge's political career thus:

> Entering law and politics in Massachusetts, he had always been competent, taciturn, and safe. The Boston police strike gave him as governor an accidental reputation for swift decision and made him Vice-President. But he had had little impact on Washington. According to a young Republican editor in Michigan named Arthur H. Vandenberg, Coolidge was "so unimpressive" that he would probably have been denied renomination.[3]

This tightly written little paragraph, unflattering to Coolidge, suggests to the reader the following chain of events: An unimpressive governor by accident became vice-president, and an unimpressive vice-president by the accident of death became president. The reader is not surprised then to be told, a bit later, that the man who was unimpressive as governor and vice-president proved to be unimpressive as president. ("As President, he dedicated himself to inactivity.")

A chain, however, is not stronger than its weakest link. By the conclusion of the above paragraph in Schlesinger's narrative, the reader has been led to believe that an unimpressive man became president through a series of accidents. (The reader may or may not be aware that the historian is simply repeating the standard interpretation of Coolidge's career offered a half century ago by Coolidge's political enemies.) But what *reasons* has the reader been

3. Ibid., pp. 56-57.

given for accepting this interpretation? There are two. First, the reputation Governor Coolidge acquired to the contrary during the Boston police strike was "accidental." Second, Arthur Vandenberg said that Coolidge was an "unimpressive" vice-president.

Let us first take notice of the adjective "accidental." Schlesinger uses it—in the face of contrary opinion—to debunk Coolidge and to establish one of the links in his chain. But the adjective in fact stands there in utter isolation, undocumented, undefended, and unexplained either in the text or in the footnotes. Is this not a curious way for an historian to treat a pivotal and hotly debated episode in a president's career? However that may be, the careful reader will be aware at this point in Schlesinger's narrative that he has only the historian's own opinion as the basis for calling Coolidge's reputation accidental.

The truth is that the Coolidge we see in Schlesinger's passing reference to the police strike is a straw man. Coolidge's reputation was not for "swift" decision but rather for firm and courageous decision. Coolidge himself, in his autobiography, notes that he did not act as swiftly as he was inclined to at the outset of the strike. But in his commitment to certain principles, including the principle of rule by law, he was absolutely unwavering before, during, and after the strike. It was this, not the speed of his actions, that made him a national hero.

Our own opinion, which we will elaborate in a subsequent chapter, is that Coolidge's conduct and reputation flowed from a fixed character; there was nothing accidental about them at all. Furthermore, we believe that Coolidge's method of speaking softly but carrying a big stick would not be inappropriate as a model for the present day, when some public employee unions have grown arrogant, surly, and assertive, heeding neither the law nor the will of the majority. Today these unions are opposed, when they are opposed at all, by bloated rhetoric and supine actions. How admirable Coolidge appears by contrast! He watched and waited, quietly and cagily. At the decisive moment he intervened decisively, taking all power into his own hands. Thereafter he was granite-like in his refusal to readmit any of the policemen who had deserted their posts, had left their city defenseless, and had thereby committed what Woodrow Wilson called a crime against civilization.

We know a man not only by his deeds but also by his words. Coolidge was far from being a Lincoln, but he did possess something of Lincoln's genius for persuasively compressing reams of argument into a sentence. Thus when challenged by Samuel Gompers, Governor Coolidge electrified the nation with his words: "There is no right to strike against the public safety by any body, any where, any time."

Coolidge's initial watchfulness, his decisive intervention, and his moral firmness in speech and deed were fixtures of his conduct, then and always. In this sense his nomination for vice-president was by no means accidental.

All we are left with then, aside from Schlesinger's own opinion, is the opinion of Arthur Vandenberg, who said that Coolidge was unimpressive as vice-president. Never mind that vice-presidents typically have little impact on Washington. (The well-known comments of two of Coolidge's contemporaries, Mr. Marshall and Mr. Garner, are sufficient to indicate the prestige of that office.) Never mind that the foothold of vice-presidents is notoriously insecure. Never mind that this is simply one man's opinion. Let us assume with our historian that Arthur Vandenberg's opinion of Coolidge is worth hearing.

It happens that Professor Schlesinger likes to get his character witnesses into the witness box and out again with dispatch. More often than not he is loath to quote even as much as a single sentence from his source; he prefers to

quote phrases or snippets. In the present example we are
left with the phrase "so unimpressive" ringing in our ears.
But this technique sometimes fails to capture the full flavor
of a more extensive quotation. Vandenberg actually had
more to say about Coolidge than comes across in Schlesinger's
account:

> Death put its tragic hand upon President Harding before his
> work was done. Succeeding him came a quiet, modest,
> unperturbable New Englander who— while so unimpressive
> as Vice-President that he probably would have been denied
> re-nomination even for second place, had his chief survived—*has
> captured the well-nigh universal imagination of the people*
> in his unruffled, common sense dependabilities in the *higher
> station* which he now occupies *in his own right*. The
> character of President Calvin Coolidge partakes the
> atmosphere of those granite hills that gave him birth. *He never
> shirks a rendezvous with duty*. He came to maturity in a
> sector of the nation which not only is rich in intimate
> tradition, but also believes in keeping green the laurel of these
> patriotic memories. *It is inevitable that all worthy tradition
> in his keeping shall be safe. It is certain that the trail will not
> wander while his compass points the onward press*. (Italics
> mine.)[4]

One must wonder what induced Schlesinger to reach
into this garish heap of accolades and pluck out the single
parenthetical fleck of dung with which to besmirch Coolidge. Fastidiousness? Scholarly rigor? Impartiality? Our
historian's selectivity puts him in the role of a prosecutor
who wrenches one damaging remark out of a witness's
mouth and then shuts him up before he can say anything
else. But now that the first witness for the prosecution has
been cross-examined let us call in the next.

In the very next paragraph Schlesinger continues to
quote fragments.

4. Arthur H. Vandenberg, *The Trail of a Tradition* (New York: G. Putnam's
Sons, 1926), p. 396.

His speeches offered his social philosophy in dry pellets of aphorism. "The chief business of the American people," he said, "is business." But, for Coolidge, business was more than business; it was a religion; and to it he committed all the passion of his arid nature. "The man who builds a factory," he wrote, "builds a temple. . . . The man who works there worships there." He felt these things with a fierce intensity. William Allen White, who knew him well, called him a mystic, a whirling dervish of business, as persuaded of the divine character of wealth as Lincoln had been of the divine character of man, "crazy about it, sincerely, genuinely, terribly crazy."[5]

"William Allen White, *who knew him well* . . ." Here is a fine phrase. It lends authority to Mr. White's opinions and justifies our historian in citing them. He knew him well. In fact, White had not been an intimate of Coolidge before he became president. "I met him," says White, "in the White House in December, 1924."[6] This was a mere fifteen months before White wrote the letter that Schlesinger quotes, during which time White and Coolidge met only twice more, and on one of those occasions they had had only a brief chat. But aside from the fact that White knew Coolidge well, what reasons are we given for respecting his opinions about Coolidge?

We may illustrate as follows the problem that the historian faces in selecting his material. Suppose that a historian were to write a short sketch of the ideas and personality of, say, Franklin Roosevelt. Suppose that he quoted from someone (there were many) who believed that Mr. Roosevelt was "unimpressive" before he became president. Suppose that he then quoted from someone who disliked Roosevelt (there were many) in order to document his vices (e.g., he was an adulterer) and his eccentricities (e.g., he

---

5. Schlesinger, *Crisis of the Old Order*, p. 57.
6. William Allen White, *A Puritan in Babylon* (New York: The Macmillan Company, 1938), p. vi.

was superstitious). Suppose that he then concluded, after a few out-of-context snippets from Roosevelt's social philosophy, with the following (authentic) quotation from William Allen White, who knew him well ("my old friend Bill White," as FDR once called him).

> He is in no sense democratic. Neither is he a free spirit. He is a bound and chained patrician who must give benevolences and issue commands—and not work with those who are trying to achieve a better social order. I think he has a God complex. Once in ancient Egypt a ruler hired his parrot to cry, "Hano is God!" all day long. It seems to me that Roosevelt with his court and his astrologers and jesters is making Hano's mistake.[7]

Apparently Roosevelt was as persuaded of the divine character of himself as Coolidge was of the divine character of wealth! What would Professor Schlesinger, winner of the Bancroft Award, winner of the Pulitzer Prize, consecrated to the historian's classical ideal of objectivity, say about such a sketch? What would anyone say?

Let us take a moment to examine White's view of Coolidge, since it is White's biography of Coolidge, more than any other, that has molded subsequent opinion about the man. In writing to a friend, White compared Coolidge to Old Scrooge:

> I didn't expect you to like the Coolidge book, and yet I do think the old man is a mystic. Old Scrooge was a mystic. He had faith in the divine character of wealth as much as Lincoln had in the divine character of man. He and Coolidge both believe that Commerce is a sacrosanct matter.[8]

---

7. William Allen White, *Selected Letters of William Allen White 1899-1943*, ed. Walter Johnson (New York: H. Holt and Company, 1947), p. 380.
8. Ibid., p. 255.

Scrooge, of course, was the mean-spirited miser who loved money for its own sake. Thus White, in the book to which he referred above, describes Coolidge as follows:

> But one can be a mystic, indeed one can be as fanatic as a dervish or a dreamer and still believe in the mysticism which *justifies business for its own sake*. Coolidge exalts the ideals of the peddler, the horse trader, the captain of industry.[9] (Italics mine.)

Coolidge has "a mystic faith in the righteousness of a swap." Coolidge "believes in the power of the esoteric and mystical qualities of business to produce a happy people." Coolidge has "faith in the Divine ordination of wealth to rule the world and promote civilized progress . . ."[10]

Schlesinger follows White: Coolidge worshipped business; business for him was a religion; Coolidge fanatically consecrated himself to the prestige of the business community. And are not White and Schlesinger supported by Coolidge's own words? "The chief business of the American people is business." What more needs to be said?

Perhaps the first thing that needs to be said is that this aphorism, much ridiculed and much maligned, is the precise truth. America *is* a commercial republic. Now, just as fifty years ago, the principal activity of the American people is business. This is *not* to say—and Coolidge *never* said—that business is the highest activity in America, or that it is pursued for its own sake, or that it will automatically secure for us the good life. Coolidge seems to be Coolidge the Philistine only because White and Schlesinger will not let him get a word in edgewise.

---

9. William Allen White, *Calvin Coolidge: The Man Who is President* (New York: The Macmillan Company, 1925), p. 218.
10. Ibid., pp. 219, 220, 224.

> After all, the chief business of the American people is
> business. They are profoundly concerned with producing,
> buying, selling, investing and prospering in the world. I am
> strongly of the opinion that the great majority of people will
> always find these are moving impulses of our life. . . .
> Wealth is the product of industry, ambition, character and
> untiring effort. In all experience, the accumulation of wealth
> means the multiplication of schools, the increase of knowledge,
> the dissemination of intelligence, the encouragement of
> science, the broadening of outlook, the expansion of liberties,
> the widening of culture. Of course, *the accumulation of
> wealth cannot be justified as the chief end of existence*. But we
> are compelled to recognize it is *a* means to well-nigh every
> desirable achievement. So long as wealth is made the means
> and not the end, we need not greatly fear it.[11] (Italics
> mine.)

Coolidge's attitude toward money-making and wealth is
the commonsensical one, namely, that wealth is justified
only as a means to higher ends. Without wealth you will
not have hospitals, schools, and museums. William Allen
White would have us believe that Coolidge thought justice
"in some occult way" would be "secreted" from the activity
of the peddler and the captain of industry. This is false.
Coolidge's clear position was that wealth cannot be accumulated or preserved, in the long run, outside of a frame-
work provided by liberal culture and the more mundane
virtues, e.g., "the homely fundamental virtue" of economy. Culture and virtue produce wealth, wealth does not
produce them. Wealth is merely a necessary, not a sufficient,
condition for progress. But wealth does provide, in its
turn, the leisure and the wherewithal to pursue, for instance,
a liberal education, which is among the noblest ends of
man.

The common sense of the matter is illustrated perfectly

---

11. Calvin Coolidge, *Foundations of the Republic* (Freeport: Books for Librar-
    ies Press, 1926; reprint ed., 1968), pp. 187-188.

by Coolidge's own background. Many a God-fearing man of sturdy character, in Coolidge's experience, had scratched a living and a little more out of the soil in order to send his son to school, where the young man could add to the virtues of character those of intellect. There is nothing esoteric or mystical about this process at all.

Nor were these mere Coolidgean platitudes, issuing from the mouth but not the heart. Coolidge himself was as well educated as any president since. Even as an adult he would spend evenings translating Cicero and Dante from the original into English. (The mind simply balks when requested to produce the image of LBJ, Nixon, and Ford hunched over their Dante.) On many occasions Coolidge wrote movingly about the poetry of Homer and Shakespeare and the Bible. He was as well a competent and facile writer of English prose, a fact attested to by many of his contemporaries, including H. L. Mencken and Charles and Mary Beard, but ignored by most recent historians. His prose is not inferior to that of any of his successors, nor is it inferior to that of most of those historians who pass him off as a philistine, a boorish celebrant of acquisitiveness. Far from exalting the ideals of the captain of industry, Coolidge again and again lamented that America was "falling away from this ideal" of a liberal education.

> Great captains of industry who have aroused the wonder of the world by their financial success would not have been captains at all had it not been for the generations of liberal culture in the past and the existence all about them of a society permeated, inspired, and led by the liberal culture of the present. If it were possible to strike out that factor from present existence, he would find all the value of his great possessions diminish to the vanishing point, and he himself would be but a barbarian among barbarians.[12]

12. Calvin Coolidge, *America's Need for Education* (Boston: Houghton Mifflin Company, 1925), p. 35.

The blessings of a free republic, including the promotion of literature and the arts,

> are not to be inquired of for gain or profit, though without them all gain and all profit would pass away. They will not be found in the teachings devoted exclusively to commercialism, though without them commerce would not exist. These are the higher things of life. Their teaching has come to us from the classics. If they are to be maintained they will find their support in the institutions of the liberal arts. When we are drawing away from them we are drawing away from the path of security and progress.[13]

Will the progress of mankind be "secreted" from the activity of the peddler? The following is the peroration of Coolidge's speech on the one hundred and fiftieth anniversary of the Declaration of Independence.

> We live in an age of science and of abounding accumulation of material things. These did not create our Declaration. Our Declaration created them. The things of the spirit come first. Unless we cling to that, all our material prosperity, overwhelming though it may appear, will turn to a barren sceptre in our grasp. If we are to maintain the great heritage which has been bequeathed to us, we must be like-minded as the fathers who created it. We must not sink into a pagan materialism. We must cultivate the reverence they had for the things that are holy.[14]

These are passages that have not found their way into the history books.

But let us return to Professor Schlesinger's narrative. In the final paragraph of his review of Coolidge's social philosophy, he makes four assertions about Coolidge. We do not apologize for reproducing the entire passage, even at the risk of wearying the reader; for we do not subscribe to the

13. Ibid., p. 57.
14. Coolidge, *Foundations*, p. 454.

cut-and-paste method of disputation. On the contrary, we relish hearing different opinions about men and policies expressed at adequate length.

> As he worshipped business, so he detested government. "If the Federal Government should go out of existence, the common run of people would not detect the difference in the affairs of their daily life for a considerable length of time." The federal government justified itself only as it served business. "The law that builds up the people is the law that builds up industry." And the chief way by which the federal government could serve business was to diminish itself; "the Government can do more to remedy the economic ills of the people by a system of rigid economy in public expenditure than can be accomplished through any other action." Economy was his self-confessed obsession; it was "idealism in its most practical form"; it was the "full test of our national character."[15]

This is Schlesinger's summary of Coolidge's social philosophy. Each assertion is "documented" with a short phrase or sentence from Coolidge himself, but in no case—except the last—do the quotations justify the charges.

Let us begin with the last charge. Schlesinger quotes Coolidge to prove that economy was his self-confessed obsession: "[Economy] was 'idealism in its most practical form;' it was the 'full test of our national character.'" It is a wary reader who will not surrender to the drift of this sentence. Coolidge does not say that economy is idealism in its only form, or its purest form, or its highest form; it is merely idealism in its most mundane, *practical* form. In context, Coolidge's aphorism is both perfectly clear and perfectly true:

> I favor the policy of economy, not because I wish to save money, but because I wish to save people. The men and

15. Schlesinger, *Crisis*, p. 57.

women of this country who toil are the ones who bear the cost
of the Government. Every dollar that we *carelessly waste*
means that their life will be so much the more meager. Every
dollar that we save means that their life will be so much the
more abundant. Economy is idealism in its most practical
form.[16] (Italics mine.)

It is the second fragment that makes the case against
Coolidge. If Coolidge had said, as Schlesinger states, that
economy "was *the* 'full test of our national character,'" then
he might justly be accused of an obsession with economy.
But Coolidge did not say that. He said that economy was "*a*
full test of our national character."[17] (Italics mine.) Only by
this small distortion can Schlesinger prove that Coolidge
had a self-confessed obsession with economy. It is necessary also for Schlesinger to omit the continuation of the
President's remarks: "I would not be misunderstood. I am
not advocating parsimony. I want to be liberal. Public
service is entitled to a suitable reward."[18]

But "at this time and under present circumstances," said
Coolidge, economy is important. He regarded it as a mani-
festation of the virtue of self-control, which lies at the heart
of self-government. Perhaps this idea was so incomprehen-
sible to our historian in 1957 that he could not do justice to
it. But the fact that economy is a full test of our national
character, and hence of self-government, is a commonplace—a platitude—in the year 1982. That there are other,
and greater, tests of national character was, of course,
known to Coolidge, and is nothing to the point.

Let us work our way through Mr. Schlesinger's other
charges. "The federal government justified itself only as it
served business." Before proceeding to an analysis of this
charge, we should caution the reader. When Coolidge

16. Coolidge, *Foundations*, p. 201.
17. Ibid., p. 41.
18. Ibid.

speaks of business he usually does not wish to be understood as speaking of a separate class with distinct interests. He usually means "the work of the world" or the commercial enterprise as a whole. "Business" for him was an all-inclusive term that included labor, farmers, businessmen, etc. If one does not know this, one is liable to be misled by fragmentary quotations.

Calvin Coolidge never said that the federal government justified itself *only* as it served "business." Schlesinger attributes this sentiment to Coolidge on the basis of the following quotation: "The law that builds up the people is the law that builds up industry." The reader may be interested to know that Schlesinger, despite his attachment to scholarly rigor, does not bother to tell us where to find this remark by Coolidge, a remark which taken out of context might as well be a Delphic oracle, for all the meaning it imparts. It happens that the remark is taken from a speech delivered in 1916,[19] and the "federal government" is not explicitly mentioned. Moreover, the "law" to which Coolidge refers is not federal legislation, nor any positive law whatsoever, but economic and social "law." There is nothing whatever in the speech about the federal government serving business. In fact, the only reference at all in the speech to the federal government is an oblique one in which Coolidge, having deplored that under the influence of prosperity "men came to think that prosperity was the chief end of man and grew arrogant in the use of its power," defends the anti-trust laws.

> They are sound in theory. Their assemblances of wealth are broken up because they were assembled for an unlawful purpose. It is the purpose that is condemned. You men who represent our industries can see that there is the same right

19. Calvin Coolidge, *Have Faith in Massachusetts*, 2d ed. (Boston: Houghton Mifflin and Company, 1919), pp. 63-68.

to disperse unlawful assembling of wealth or power that there
is to disperse a mob that has met to lynch or riot.[20]

Professor Schlesinger, far from exerting himself to mas-
ter his own partisan passions, has dug up an obscure sentence from Coolidge, has refused to tell his readers where
he got it, has used it to prove something that it does not
prove either by itself or in its original context, and has
ignored an explicit assertion by Coolidge, not that the
federal government exists only to serve business, but that
the government exists in part to regulate, to check, and to
discipline business.

Professor Schlesinger's Coolidge is a man who sometimes advocated a laissez-faire attitude toward government,
so as to give business a free rein, and who sometimes
advocated special government privileges for business, e.g.,
the tariff. The unifying motivation for this two-faced Coolidge, that which makes his political career a consistent
whole, is his devotion to business. As Schlesinger put it in
The Vital Center:

> The Progressive bolt left the plutocracy in unchallenged
> control of Republicanism. Never in American history have
> any administrations served the business community so
> faithfully—one might say so obsequiously—as the Republi-
> can administrations of Harding, Coolidge, and Hoover.[21]

Schlesinger defines plutocracy as "a possessing class founded, not upon the complex values of status which arise in a
stable and independent society, but on the naked accumulation of money."[22] Coolidge's presidency, therefore, was
in the service of the naked accumulation of money.

20. Ibid., p. 65.
21. Arthur M. Schlesinger, Jr., *The Vital Center* (Boston: Houghton Mifflin
    Company, 1962), p. 24.
22. Ibid., p. 13.

Professor Schlesinger has every right to make this argument. He is free to try to prove that Coolidge was a conscious or unconscious hypocrite, that he said one thing and did another. But he is *not* free to assert that Coolidge articulated his political principles as Schlesinger articulates them. Coolidge never claimed to be the servant of the business class or the plutocracy. He was not "crazy" about wealth. He never claimed to worship business, or to detest government, or to believe that government exists only to serve business. Mr. Schlesinger splices quotations, he changes words, he quotes out of context, he offers up irrelevant bits and pieces—all this to condemn Coolidge out of Coolidge's own mouth. But the real Calvin Coolidge is not the man we see after he has been filtered through the imagination of our historians. Schlesinger would have us believe that business was running the country in the twenties and that agriculture, labor, and other groups were outside the orbit of the business classes. Here is Schlesinger's Coolidge confirming this analysis on page 61 of *The Crisis of the Old Order:*

> "Never before, here or anywhere else," added the *Wall Street Journal*, "has a government been so completely fused with business." From his side, Calvin Coolidge confirmed the alliance. "This is a business country," he said, " . . . and it wants a business government."

Why is the ellipsis there? Why did our historian quote only a single sentence from the president? Was it from a desire to make his diagnosis more complex? Here is the real Coolidge:

> This is a business country, pre-eminent in all kinds of business, industrial *and* agricultural, and it wants a business government.
> I do *not* mean by that a government *by* business, nor a

government *for* business, but I do mean a government that
will *understand* business. I mean a government able to
establish the best possible relations between the *people* in
their business capacity and the people in their social
capacity.[23] (Italics mine.)

Did Coolidge himself ever say that government and
business were "fused" or that they had formed an "alliance"? The following is a sample of his thoughts on that
very possibility.

When we contemplate the enormous power, autocratic and
uncontrolled, which would have been created by joining the
authority of government with the influence of business, we
can better appreciate the wisdom of the fathers in their wise
dispensation which made Washington the political center of
the country and left New York to develop into its business
center. . . . When government comes unduly under the
influence of business, the tendency is to develop an administration
which closes the door of opportunity; becomes narrow and
selfish in its outlook, and results in oligarchy. When government enters the field of business with great resources, it has
a tendency to extravagance and inefficiency, but, having the
power to crush all competitors, likewise closes the door of
opportunity and results in monopoly.[24]

Call the man a hypocrite—if you think you can prove
it—but do not ascribe to him sentiments which he never
uttered.

"As he worshipped business, so he detested government."
The quotation from Coolidge that allegedly proves this
assertion is as follows: "If the Federal Government should
go out of existence, the common run of people would not
detect the difference in the affairs of their daily life for a
considerable length of time." Where in this sentence is

23. *New York Times,* October 24, 1924.
24. Coolidge, *Foundations,* pp. 317-319.

there anything about detesting government? On its face
the sentence fails to accomplish the task Schlesinger assigns
it. Coolidge is simply stating a fact, namely, that under the
federal system (as it then stood) the states were more
intimately involved with the daily affairs of the people than
was the federal government. In context this is obvious, but
once again our historian fails to supply us with the context,
and once again he conveniently fails to footnote the quotation, so that the reader might consider the context for
himself.

> . . . the States are the sheet anchors of our institutions. If the
> Federal Government should go out of existence, the
> common run of people would not detect the difference in the
> affairs of their daily life for a considerable length of time.
> But if the authority of the States were struck down disorder
> approaching chaos would be upon us in twenty-four hours.[25]

To say that certain governmental powers are best exer-
cised at the state or local level may be wrong, but it is
surely not the equivalent of detesting government as such.
Moreover, by speaking of the states as the sheet anchors of
our institutions, Coolidge implies that the Union is the
main anchor of those institutions. As he said later in the
same speech, the Union is "the source from which the
States derive their chief title to fame . . ."

> . . .when the great body of public opinion of the Nation
> requires action the States ought to understand that unless
> they are responsive to such sentiment the national authority
> will be compelled to intervene. The doctrine of State rights
> is not a privilege to continue in wrong-doing but a privilege to
> be free from interference in well-doing.[26]

25. Ibid., p. 410.
26. Ibid., p. 411.

During his political service in Massachusetts, Coolidge was not a member of the Old Guard; he was a mild progressive. He was by no means a rigid ideological opponent of government. He did believe, when president, that prudence required strong emphasis upon economy and tax reduction in the aftermath of World War I. But as a prudent man he also knew that other circumstances might justify opposite policies. For example, Coolidge spoke of taxes at Riverside during the Massachusetts state campaign of 1916.

> Good government cannot be found at the bargain counter. . . .
> We cannot curtail the usual appropriations or the care of
> mothers with dependent children or the support of the poor,
> the insane, and the infirm. . . . Our party will have no part
> in a scheme of economy which adds to the misery of the wards
> of the Commonwealth—the sick, the insane, and the
> unfortunate; those who are too weak even to protest.
>   Because I know these conditions I know a Republican
> administration would face an increasing State tax rather than
> not see them remedied.[27]

This was the man who detested government.

*   *   *

> One must emphasize, however, that this duty of
> [historical] judgment applies to *issues*. Because we are all
> implicated in the same tragedy, we must judge the men of the
> past with the same forbearance and charity which we hope
> the future will apply toward us.[28]

Professor Schlesinger was not content to set forth Coolidge's political opinions. He proceeded from the issues to a presentation of Coolidge's character:

27. Coolidge, *Have Faith,* pp. 38-40.
28. Arthur M. Schlesinger, Jr., "The Causes of the Civil War," *Partisan Review,* October 1949, p. 981.

> As President, he dedicated himself to inactivity. "No other President in my time," said the White House usher, "ever slept so much." In his dozen or so waking hours, he did as little as possible.

It is moving to see our historian so filled with the spirit of charity. He is no less filled with the spirit of precision. The White House usher had said that Coolidge slept an average of eleven hours a day. Schlesinger amends this to a "dozen or so." But Schlesinger also implies that one can tell how hard Coolidge worked ("he dedicated himself to inactivity") on the basis of how long he slept. This conclusion, however, does not emerge from the account given by the White House usher. The usher says that Coolidge could be found in the Executive Office three or four times a day on Sundays and holidays, and he confirms Coolidge's claim that he worked there in the evenings as well. (Woodrow Wilson, in contrast, never worked on Saturday or Sunday, and before the war he never worked more than three or four hours a day.) But why did not Mr. Schlesinger seize on this opportunity to quote William Allen White, who knew Coolidge well? White said that Coolidge at fifty-nine looked like a man of seventy. "The impact of his Presidential responsibilities had weighted him down."[29] White quoted Mrs. Coolidge: "The death of our younger son was a severe shock and the zest of living never was the same to him afterward."[30] Others have speculated that Coolidge, who never enjoyed robust health, long suffered from a heart condition that drained his strength. Whatever the cause, Coolidge aged greatly during his presidency. If he had chosen to serve another term he would have died in office. It goes without saying that most historians, despite these facts, depict Coolidge as a man who hibernated for five years in the White House.

29. White, *Puritan*, p. 428.
30. Ibid., p. 434.

President Coolidge carried himself with dignity. He had the reputation of a man of character. William Allen White, who knew him well, has set down some of his impressions of Mr. Coolidge:

> Here was a shy man . . . here was a kindly man, grateful and sentimental . . . here was a trained mind; a studious, competent man, tenacious of facts, and capable of coordinating them into a hypothesis that made truth as he saw it . . . here was a man whose social graces were not formal, but were based upon an instinctive desire to be pleasant rather than punctilious . . . here was a gentle and loyal friend.[31]

We appeal to a candid audience, of whatever political persuasion. In the following description of Coolidge by Schlesinger, which is based largely upon the observations of the White House usher, are *any* of Coolidge's admirable traits in evidence? Or is not the whole effect of the paragraph to strip Coolidge of whatever dignity he possessed, to reveal him as mean, eccentric, and ridiculous?

> The main social events at the White House in Coolidge's time were his breakfasts: pancakes with Vermont maple syrup, served promptly at eight, his large white collies wandering about the room or licking the sugar out of the bottom of his coffee cup. On other mornings, he ate breakfast in his bedroom while a valet rubbed his head with vaseline. When his faith was not involved, he watched life with a quizzical air. His humor was mordant and unpredictable. His eyes sometimes shone with the peculiar gleam of a parrot about to give someone a tweak; and then deadly remarks snapped out of compressed lips; or, in a mood of aimless mischief, he might play unfunny practical jokes on the Secret Service men. He could be irascible and nasty, straining all the understanding of his gracious wife. In the memory of the White House usher, Theodore Roosevelt in his worst rage was placid compared with Coolidge.

31. Ibid., p. xiii.

"The main social events at the White House . . ." One suspects that this is supposed to be a joke. If so, it is as unfunny as some of Coolidge's pranks. Needless to say, the main social events at the Coolidge White House were the usual ones, and the Coolidges were the hosts for a glamorous succession of notables, from the Queen of England to the Queen of Rumania, from the Prince of Wales to Lindbergh. As for Coolidge's humor, it was the opinion of William Allen White, who knew him well, that Coolidge had a fine sense of humor. If Mr. Schlesinger may cite the White House usher, certainly it ought to be permitted to cite the White House maid!

> I used to ask Mama if the President were really as stern and sour-faced as he looked in pictures, and she would assure me that he was not.
> "That's just his way, and he has the public fooled," she said, "but he has the best sense of humor and makes more people laugh than any of the other Presidents I've known."[32]

Humor, no doubt, is one of those subjects upon which opinions can differ. Coolidge's practical jokes, for example, may not be to everyone's taste, though they were surely less juvenile and less sadistic than, say, pushing someone into a swimming pool in full evening dress. It all depends on your point of view.

"He could be irascible and nasty, straining all the understanding of his gracious wife." This is one of our favorite lines in Professor Schlesinger's entire corpus, but not just because it gives us an especially flat glimpse of cardboard Coolidge. Rather it is one of those marvelous criticisms which as stated would apply equally well to every married man in the history of the world, with the possible exception of Mr. Schlesinger himself. Since he has cast the first stone

32. Lillian Rogers Parks, *My Thirty Years Backstairs at the White House* (New York: Fleet Publishing, 1961), p. 178.

we must assume him to be without sin. After all, Mr.
Schlesinger, as we know, judges the men of the past with
the same forbearance and charity with which he hopes the
future will judge him. But the rest of us, who have on
occasion strained the understanding of our gracious wives,
would be edified to know that there was another side to
Coolidge, a side that we could find out about by reading
William Allen White, who knew Coolidge well:

> Here is a flash into the heart of Calvin Coolidge, irritable
> probably, peevish sometimes, not above the petty cruelties of
> a repressed and sublimated inner wrath, but still always
> loyal, always deeply affectionate and through it all profoundly
> devoted. In the various loyalties of Calvin Coolidge, and he
> had many and they were strong, none was more beautiful than
> his loyalty to this woman.[33]

"In the memory of the White House usher . . ." At long
last we begin to weary of this usher. If Coolidge had been
president in distant antiquity, if the records of that age had
been lost, if this book by the White House usher were the
only surviving record of that age, would we not regret the
sparseness of the historical record, and would we not exercise great caution in our judgment of Coolidge? What could
be said of an historian who, having at his disposal a diverse
cache of documents from that distant age, chose to ignore
them, and instead based his portrait of Coolidge upon the
churlish recollections of the White House usher? If only
Professor Schlesinger had profited more from his reading
of Hegel.

> These psychologists are particularly fond of contemplating
> those peculiarities of great historical figures which appertain
> to them as private persons. Man must eat and drink; he
> sustains relations to friends and acquaintances; he has
> passing impulses and ebullitions of temper. "No man is a hero
> to his valet-de-chambre," is a well-known proverb; I have

33. White, *Puritan*, p. 438.

added—and Goethe repeated it ten years later—"not because the former is no hero, but because the latter is a valet." He takes off the hero's boots, assists him to bed, knows that he prefers champagne, etc. Historical personages waited upon in historical literature by such psychological valets, come poorly off; they are brought down by their attendants to a level with—or rather a few degrees below the level of—the morality of such exquisite discerners of spirits.[34]

Throughout his career Professor Schlesinger has inveighed against the intrusion of ideology into the political consciousness. Ideology, he contends, is unfaithful to the richness and diversity of the political phenomena. But what is Mr. Schlesinger himself if not the incarnation of ideology? American conservatism, he tells us again and again, is typically animated by selfish, short-sighted anti-social greed. American history is the continuing struggle between the plutocrats—the forces of darkness—and the people.

To the non-ideologue it is unclear at first how Calvin Coolidge would fit into such a cramped interpretation. Whatever the ultimate merits of his political opinions and policies, Coolidge was a decent and dignified man, as learned as any president since, intensely patriotic, and possessed of a profoundly democratic soul. The people elected him to office every time save one that he presented himself for their judgment. The people elected him president by an enormous majority.

But if the man does not readily fit into a cast-iron interpretation of American history, he certainly will after Procrustes is through with him. A bit of chopping, a bit of stretching, and Coolidge appears as a mean little philistine, a high priest of the golden calf, a willing tool of the plutocracy, a whirling dervish of business, a bleak fanatic, arid, smug, self-centered and self-satisfied, irascible and nasty. Such is the craftsmanship of a prize-winning historian.

34. G. W. F. Hegel, *The Philosophy of History* (New York: Dover Publications, Inc., 1966), p. 32.

Two

The Boston Police Strike

Calvin Coolidge emerged a national hero from the Boston police strike of 1919. The following year he was nominated spontaneously for vice-president by the Republican national convention, and three years after that, upon the death of Warren Harding, he became the thirtieth president of the United States. The Boston police strike was the only spectacular episode in the steadiest and most unspectacular climb to the top of the political ladder in American history.

Coolidge's reputation in the police strike has paralleled his reputation more generally. It reached an early zenith and has been sinking ever since. Well might Coolidge have said, with Wolsey:

> I have touch'd the highest point of all my greatness;
> And, from that full meridian of my glory,
> I haste now to my setting. I shall fall
> Like a bright exhalation in the evening,
> And no man see me more.

In the years following the strike Coolidge was lionized by a succession of adulatory biographers. Dissenting from the popular view were periodicals such as the *Nation*, the *New Republic*, and the *American Mercury*. In their view Coolidge was a timid, hesitant, cautious man who had done his best to steer clear of the police strike, who had refused to take any action to prevent the strike or protect the city of Boston, and who had foisted the responsibility for the hard

decisions onto the shoulders of others. But once the back of
the strike was broken and public opinion had asserted itself
decisively against the strikers, Coolidge belatedly acted
and by a stroke of luck received the lion's share of the glory
for putting down the strike. "So," said Randolph Bartlett in
the *American Mercury*, "the chronicle of blunders ends on
the ironic note of Coolidge calling out the Guard when
fighting was finished and order had been restored."[1] Said
the *Nation*, in an article entitled, "Calvin Coolidge: Made
by a Myth,"

> Governor Coolidge sat discreetly on the fence until he saw
> on which side public sentiment was gathering. When this had
> manifested itself distinctly against the police, and after
> Boston's danger had been averted, Governor Coolidge climbed
> down from the fence on the side with the crowd and issued
> a bombastic proclamation needlessly mobilizing the entire
> State Guard.[2]

What once was a commonplace to the readers of the
Nation has now become a commonplace to American historians. In 1975 Francis Russell published a little book about
the police strike entitled *A City in Terror*. The book was an
enlargement of an earlier article by Russell in which he had
summarized Coolidge's role in the strike as follows: "Ironically
enough, Coolidge, who did the least, received the final
credit for doing everything."[3] Reviewing Russell's book in
the *National Review*, Aram Bakshian, Jr. voiced the current opinion of Coolidge's conduct: "His 'firm' stand, actually taken only after an initial period of *almost criminal*

1. Randolph Bartlett, "Anarchy in Boston," *American Mercury*, December
   1935, p. 464.
2. "Calvin Coolidge: Made by a Myth," *Nation*, August 15, 1923, p. 153.
3. Francis Russell, "The Strike that Made a President," *American Heritage*,
   October 1963, p. 45.
4. Aram Bakshian, Jr., "An Unhappy Lot," *National Review*, July 18, 1975,
   p. 781.

neglect, catapulted Coolidge to nationwide fame.["]4 (Italics mine.)

The other two principals in the 1919 police strike, Police Commissioner Edwin Curtis and Mayor Andrew J. Peters, have, if anything, fared even worse than Coolidge in the history books. Curtis is generally portrayed as a stern, uncompromising autocrat, whose unreasonable stubbornness goaded the oppressed policemen into striking. The reputation of Mayor Peters has not been helped by the subsequent revelation that he was possessed by an uncontrollable lust for pubescent girls. Apart from that character defect, he was, according to historians, a playboy, a part-time mayor, and a womanish man who at the moment of greatest danger to his city showed himself to be weak, frightened, and hysterical.

Our own research has not led us to such harsh judgments against any of the principals. On the contrary we find ourselves empathizing with each man as he tried to make his way through one of those dark, tangled, and confusing thickets that are hateful to any man of good will. "The requirements of the situation as it developed seem clear and plain now, and easy to decide," wrote Calvin Coolidge a decade after the event, "but as they arose they were very complicated and involved in many immaterial issues."[5] The quiet implication of this sentence is that it required an act of statesmanship to cut through the immaterial issues to the heart of the matter, and to reveal the heart of the matter to the citizens of Massachusetts and of America. Whether subsequent historiography has itself become ensnared in a thicket of immaterial issues is one of the questions we must consider.

In this essay we intend to conduct a dialogue with Gover-

5. Calvin Coolidge, *The Autobiography of Calvin Coolidge* (New York, Cosmopolitan Book Corporation, 1929), p. 135.

nor Coolidge's critics about the course of the Boston police
strike. Our chief interlocutor in this discussion will be
Professor Donald McCoy, a recent biographer of Coolidge
(*Calvin Coolidge, The Quiet President*).[6] Professor McCoy
has written a pedestrian biography of a man whom he
obviously regards as a pedestrian president. But the merit
of McCoy's book is that it attempts to make a fair assessment of Coolidge. McCoy steers between the praise heaped
upon Coolidge by his early biographers and the universal
condemnation of him by later historians.

In his chapter on the Boston police strike McCoy lends
his authority to the belief that Coolidge reaped undeserved
credit from the strike. The chapter ends with this sentence:
"He who had been the last in acting had become the first in
receiving credit."[7] Professor McCoy makes three specific
charges against Coolidge. First, he charges that Governor
Coolidge repeatedly refused to intervene to break the deadlock between Commissioner Curtis and the Boston police,
and that "the governor's aloofness was inexcusable." Second, McCoy downplays Coolidge's support of Curtis, stating that the governor supported the commissioner's authority "passively at first and later through timid action . . ."
Finally, McCoy charges that Coolidge, when he did finally
act during the strike, did so belatedly. ("Yet Coolidge
waited through another night of troubles before standing
on his principles.") Nevertheless, when he did act the
fabled Coolidge luck was with him.

> For Coolidge it was a stroke of luck. The governor, not the
> mayor, would receive credit for restoring order in Boston.
> The governor, not the police commissioner, would receive
> most of the credit for upholding the principle that the sole
> allegiance of policemen should be to the public.[8]

6. Donald McCoy, *Calvin Coolidge, The Quiet President* (New York: The
   Macmillan Company, 1967).
7. Ibid., p. 94.
8. Ibid., pp. 88, 92, 91, 92.

Let us begin at the beginning and proceed chronologically through the events of August and September 1919. Everyone agrees that by 1919 the working conditions and the pay of the Boston police had become scandalous. The policemen worked eighty and ninety hour weeks. Their station houses were filthy, decrepit, and filled with roaches. Their pay scale had been established in 1898, implemented only in 1913, and was unchanged until 1919. "Understand," said Governor Coolidge the day before the strike, "that I do not approve of any strike. But can you blame the police for feeling as they do when they get less than a street car conductor?"[9]

Professor McCoy notes that both Curtis and Coolidge sympathized with the policemen. He notes further that the police received a $200 yearly pay raise in May 1919. "Yet," McCoy continues,

> this did not go far in meeting either the requests or the needs of the policemen. Their hours remained long, their working conditions deplorable, and their pay raise fell short of the increases in the cost of living. Their demands for further relief were neglected.
>
> With a deep sense of frustration, the police officers decided to take an unusual step to secure their goals. They had a local organization, the Boston Social Club, which became the vehicle for their efforts to get help. In June, 1919, the Club made tentative plans to affiliate with the American Federation of Labor, in the hope that a unionized police force, with organized labor's support, would be more successful in bargaining with public officials. Although the police in some other cities had joined the AFL and although there was no specific law or rule against affiliation in Boston, Commissioner Curtis' reaction was hostile. He was not going to deal with his men through a labor union. Curtis was an honest official and he tried to be fair. But as one of his admirers, Sherwin Cook, pointed out, he was "a stiff-necked executive." The commissioner would do his best for his men, but they were

9. Ibid., p. 88.

> not going to tell him what to do or how to do it. He told the
> policemen that "a police officer cannot consistently belong
> to a union and perform his sworn duty." He subsequently
> issued orders banning membership in any state or national
> organization that might get involved in labor questions.[10]

The whole effect of this passage is to portray the police
sympathetically, to suggest that their affiliation with the
AFL was neither unprecedented nor unreasonable, and to
cast Commissioner Curtis as inflexibly hostile to the not
unreasonable demands of his men. Throughout the entire
chapter Professor McCoy utters not a sentence, not a sylla-
ble, of criticism of the Boston police. And yet he refers to
Commissioner Curtis as stiff-necked and as "intransigent,"
which Webster defines as "refusing to compromise or to
abandon an extreme position." Governor Coolidge's "refusal
to urge a change of direction" upon Curtis, McCoy finds to
be inexcusable, which implies that compromise, not intransigence, would have been a reasonable response to the
policemens' demands.

Whatever may be said about Commissioner Curtis's refusal
to compromise with his men on the terms set down by the
Storrow Committee—to which we shall come shortly—he
surely cannot be condemned as "stiff-necked" merely for his
initial reaction to the proposal for affiliation with the AFL.
For this was a point upon which *no responsible official was
willing to compromise*. Governor Coolidge opposed police
affiliation with any outside body. So did Mayor Peters. So
did Mr. Storrow and his committee. So did every newspa-
per in Boston. *And so did the AFL itself, right up to the
second week in June 1919*. It would hardly be fair to single
out Curtis as "stiff-necked" for rejecting a proposal that the
AFL itself had opposed for years and that was opposed by
nearly every leading citizen in Boston.

10. Ibid., pp. 84-85.

Professor McCoy implies that there was precedent for such outside affiliation because "police in some other cities had joined the AFL." Of course a widespread practice is not justified merely because it is widespread. If, for example, many cities had autocratic police commissioners, this would not justify the presence of one in Boston. Precedent proves nothing. But in fact there was not even precedent. All the police unions to which McCoy refers had sprung into existence since June 1919. Boston was only the thirteenth city to be granted an AFL police union charter, and it was clear that this was to be a test case for other cities.

Moreover, McCoy states that "there was no specific law or rule against affiliation in Boston . . ." But he fails to mention General Order Number 129, issued by Police Commissioner O'Meara on June 28, 1918:

> It is probable that the printed rumors to the effect that members of the police department are discussing the advisability of organizing a union to be affiliated with the American Federation of Labor represent no substantial sentiment existing among them. Under ordinary conditions no attention would be paid to such rumors, but even though unfounded, they are so likely to injure the discipline, efficiency, and even the good name of the force, and the times are so favorable to the creation of discontent among men who are bearing their share of the war burdens, though still at home, that I feel it my duty to make the situation clear.
>
> There is no substantial disagreement as to the wisdom and even the necessity of maintaining unions among persons following the same industrial occupations.
>
> Though a union of public employees, as distinct from those composed of employees of private concerns, is in itself a matter of doubtful propriety, such union in any case and at the worst could affect the operations only of a particular branch of the city service. The police department, on the other hand, exists for the impartial enforcement of the laws, and protection of persons and property under all conditions. Should its members incur obligations to an outside

organization, they would be justly suspected of abandoning the impartial attitude which heretofore has vindicated their good faith as against the complaints almost invariably made by both sides in many controversies.

It is assumed erroneously that agents of an outside organization could obtain for the police advantages in pay and regulations. This is not a question of compelling a private employer to surrender a part of his profits; it has to do with police service which is wholly different from any other service, public or private—a service regulated by laws which hold to a strict responsibility certain officials, of whom the Police Commissioner is one. The policemen are their own best advocates, and to suppose that an official would yield on points of pay or regulation to the arguments or threats of an outside organization if the policemen themselves had failed to establish their case would be to mark him as cowardly and unfit for his position.

I cannot believe that a proposition to turn the police force into a union, subject to the rules and direction of any organization outside the police department will ever be presented formally to its members, but if, unfortunately, such a question should ever arise, I trust that it will be answered with an emphatic refusal by the members of the force who have an intelligent regard for their own self-respect, the credit of the department and the obligations to the whole public which they undertook with their oath of office.[11]

On July 29, 1919, Commissioner Curtis reiterated his predecessor's order, and two weeks later he added Rule 35, Section 19 to the official rules and regulations of the department. This rule explicitly banned membership in outside organizations and was later upheld by the Massachusetts courts.

The police, amply forewarned, not only by Mr. Curtis but by his predecessor as well, defied the orders of their superiors, broke the rules of their department, and disre-

11. *The Boston Police Strike: Two Reports* (New York: Arno Press and *The New York Times*, 1971), pp. 8-9.

garded the will of the elected representatives of the people of Boston. But no word of censure escapes from Professor McCoy's lips. His lips are sealed, and he opens them only to criticize nearly everyone involved in the police strike except the police. When it comes to the lawbreakers themselves, his critical faculties lapse, his indignation is stilled, and he becomes, for all practical purposes, Donald McCoy, the quiet historian.

The policemen of Boston went ahead with their plan to affiliate with the AFL. They requested a local charter, which they received on August fifteenth. Soon thereafter Commissioner Curtis charged nineteen leaders of the union with violating his orders and found them guilty as charged. But he deferred sentencing the men, as an incentive for them to come back into the fold from which they had strayed. One might suppose that such a conciliatory gesture would have softened the criticism of Curtis as an autocrat. It has not always done so. When Curtis prohibits the men from joining the AFL—a prohibition applauded even by those most sympathetic to the police—he is labeled "stiff-necked." As Ralph Bartlett said:

> He was stiff-necked as an old-time Salem pastor and stubborn as a horse mackerel. When informed that the police club proposed affiliation with the A. F. of L., he issued an order forbidding any member of the force to join, under pain of dismissal.
> This was the Curtis method—the challenge of the mailed fist.[12]

Yet when Curtis withholds draconian punishment, he provokes the following commentary from Bartlett:

> The trial of the . . . police culprits was brief and formal; all were found guilty of violating the Commissioner's order. But

12. Bartlett, "Anarchy in Boston," p. 457.

to the surprise of everyone, they were not sentenced to be
drawn and quartered on the spot. Instead, Curtis postponed
judgment for ten days—an act which has never been
explained. [Actually Curtis did explain it in his annual report
for 1919, which Bartlett obviously had not read.] Certainly
he had decided to dismiss the men, yet at the moment when
blunt steps might have won the day, he failed to exercise
his power.[13]

The commissioner simply cannot win. Unfortunately for
Bartlett, in suggesting that blunt steps might have won the
day he forgets what he has just said on the previous page:

> The fact that the majority of the policemen were of Celtic
> origin should have forewarned him that they were not to be
> moved by threats. It was a knockdown fight they were
> spoiling for, and the Commissioner's manifesto convinced them
> that only by fighting could they attain their goal.[14]

Professor McCoy will have nothing to do with such
foolishness. He states correctly that Curtis found the men
guilty, "but deferred sentencing as a lure for the leaders to
dissolve their ties with the AFL."[15] When Curtis finally did
sentence the men on September eighth—the day before
the strike—he merely suspended rather than discharged
them; even at that late date he was looking toward their
reinstatement.

Professor McCoy's chief complaint against Commissioner
Curtis is his unwillingness to agree to the compromise
recommended by the Storrow Committee. The Storrow
Committee was appointed in late August by Mayor Peters
in the hope that it could break the deadlock between the
commissioner and his men and prevent the threatened
strike. The committee was composed of thirty-four leading

13. *Ibid.*, p. 458.
14. *Ibid.*, p. 457.
15. McCoy, *Coolidge,* p. 85.

citizens of Boston. Its chairman was James Storrow, an investment banker. McCoy discusses the work of the committee and summarizes its compromise proposal:

> The citizen's committee found, as Storrow said, that it had been "brought into opposition with a man [Curtis] who, maintaining rigidly the official point of view, dealt in ultimatums."
>
> The Storrow Committee was developing a plan which it hoped would bring a peaceful and reasonable solution of the problem. The plan called for the appointment of a committee of three citizens acceptable to the police commissioner, the mayor, and the Boston policemen. That committee would study and report publicly on police wages, hours, and conditions. *As a concession to Curtis, questions of discipline would not be considered.* Affiliation with the AFL and recognition of the right to strike were out of the question, though there would be no objection to the police officers having their own local organization. Curtis refused to consider the plan.[16] (Italics mine.)

The plan of the Storrow Committee as McCoy outlines it here consisted of these elements: (1) a local union, (2) no affiliation with the AFL, and (3) a committee to study the policemen's grievances, excluding questions of discipline. This plan Curtis refused to consider, and Coolidge, albeit "timidly," backed him in that refusal. Their attitude McCoy regards as inexcusable.

Even the dullest reader must sense that the quiet historian has not told the story of the compromise as fully as he might have. Governor Coolidge, according to McCoy himself, had a good labor record. The year 1919 had been one of many bitter strikes. ". . . industrial disturbances became epidemic."

"Massachusetts under Coolidge had met the situation

16. Ibid., p. 86.

fairly well. Hysteria had been kept under control and the administration had worked to meet labor's legitimate grievances."[17]

Coolidge had intervened to help settle previous strikes during the spring and summer. He was especially anxious to maintain his good relations with labor because of his impending campaign for re-election. Claude Fuess, Coolidge's official biographer, said that one word from Coolidge would probably have ended the strike *but that word he would not utter*. He would not utter it in spite of his good record, in spite of his sympathy with labor, and in spite of his hope of re-election. The Storrow compromise was supported by the mayor of Boston, leading citizens of both parties, and every leading Boston paper save one. Francis Russell asserts that the plan was also supported by Murray Crane. Under the circumstances, Coolidge, by uttering a single word, would have made himself the man of the hour. He would have placated labor, averted the strike, and won accolades from all sides. Instead, as McCoy says, Coolidge "in effect backed Commissioner Curtis' intransigent position. . . . And from the available evidence it appears that *this was Coolidge's intention*."[18] (Italics mine.) And Coolidge did so, in his own opinion, at mortal peril to his political career.

In McCoy's account of the Boston police strike there is no extended explanation of Coolidge's motives, and the reader correctly infers from the evidence furnished by McCoy, that Coolidge's conduct was either utterly baffling or utterly indefensible. But in fact the specific reason why Curtis and Coolidge refused the compromise is very simple and very clear. It is the only reason mentioned by Curtis in his final letter to Mayor Peters before the strike, in which he rejected the compromise. This reason, as Coolidge said

17. Ibid., p. 83.
18. Ibid., p. 88.

in his *Autobiography,* was "the heart of the whole controversy . . ."[19] Whether Curtis and Coolidge were on the
right side of the controversy is a question we will be at
pains to answer. But that they were standing on a matter of
principle cannot be denied and would have been clearer in
McCoy's account if he had explicitly stated, which he did
not, point number five of the Storrow plan: "(5) That no
member of the Boston Policemen's Union should be dis-
criminated against because of any previous affiliation with
the American Federation of Labor."[20] In other words: There
shall be no discipline against the nineteen men who were
guilty of breaking the rules of the department and defying
the commissioner. The men would have directly challenged
the authority of the commissioner with impunity. To this
Curtis would not agree. Nor would Coolidge:

> When the policemen's union persisted in its course I was
> urged by a committee appointed by the Mayor to interfere and
> attempt to make Commissioner Curtis settle the dispute by
> arbitration. . . . I did not see how it was possible to arbitrate
> the question of the authority of the law, or of the necessity
> of obedience to the rules of the Department and the orders of
> the Commissioner. These principles were the heart of the
> whole controversy and the only important questions at issue. It
> can readily be seen how important they were and what the
> effect might have been if they had not been maintained. I
> decided to support them whatever the consequences might
> be. I fully expected it would result in my defeat in the coming
> campaign for reelection as Governor.[21]

Despite Curtis's reputation as a martinet, it is not to be
supposed that the nineteen offending officers would have

19. Coolidge, *Autobiography,* p. 128.
20. "Report of the Citizen's Committee Appointed by Mayor Peters to Consider the Police Situation," Appendix p. 16, *The Boston Police Strike: Two
Reports.*
21. Coolidge, *Autobiography,* pp. 127-128.

been treated harshly if they had abandoned what everyone regarded as an improper affiliation with the AFL. Curtis deliberately did not discharge them—as had been expected—because he held out hopes for their reinstatement. Coolidge echoed the commissioner's sentiments in a telegram sent to the state AFL before the strike: "I earnestly hope circumstances may arise which will cause the police officers to be reinstated."[22]

McCoy does mention the question of discipline in his summary of the compromise. ("As a concession to Curtis, questions of discipline would not be considered.") But how was Curtis to understand this "concession" except as an assurance that there would be no interference on a matter of discipline *in the future* if only he would accede to interference on a matter of discipline here and now?

An analogy may put the "concession" and the "compromise" as a whole in perspective. Let us suppose an impasse between a general and his underpaid, overworked conscripts, whose duty is to protect the country against external threats just as it is the duty of policemen to protect the citizens against internal threats.[23] Suppose that Congress has not adequately dealt with the legitimate grievances of the soldiers, who proceed to affiliate with the AFL against the explicit orders of their commanding general (upheld by the Supreme Court) and against the wishes of the President, the Congress, and the citizens. If they persisted in their disobedience surely no reasonable person would fault the general for initiating disciplinary action against them. Presumably no one would condemn him as stiff-necked. Now suppose that the soldiers, having resorted to one

22. McCoy, *Coolidge,* p. 88.
23. "In my judgment the obligation of a policeman is as sacred and as direct as the obligation of a soldier." Woodrow Wilson, quoted in Claude Fuess, *Calvin Coolidge, the Man from Vermont* (Boston: Little Brown and Company, 1940), p. 223.

illegal tactic already, announced that unless their demands were met they would attempt to gain them by yet another illegal act. Suppose that they threatened to desert their missiles, bombers, and submarines, leaving their country defenseless. Would it at that point be an act of statesmanship for the President, even upon the recommendation of a distinguished committee of citizens, to mediate between general and troops as if between equals, and to pressure the general into agreeing to the lesser demands of the men, without prejudice to them, in return for which the men would give up their only two bargaining chips (affiliation and the strike) *to which they had no right in the first place?* Is there any historian who would regard this as a reasonable "compromise?"[24]

Mayor Peters and the city either had not been able to, or would not, rectify the grievances of the police through the normal democratic process, but they were willing to consider those grievances in the face of a threat to abandon the city to human predators. What historian will endorse this appeal from the rule of law to the rule of might? To the best of our knowledge no historian has ever challenged Governor Coolidge's statement that there is no right to strike against the public safety. What then will historians say to justify their criticism of the intransigence of Curtis and Coolidge? That there is no right to strike against the public safety, but that there *is* a right to achieve one's ends by threatening such a strike? Surely Mr. McCoy would not wish to take the burden of such an argument upon himself.

24. The analogy is imperfect in two respects. First, the Boston police were not conscripts and were free to take their labor elsewhere at any moment if they felt that their plight was too oppressive. Second, the police *had* received in the spring of 1919 a $200 pay increase, *which had been their maximum demand*. The city had originally offered them much less. The new Commissioner, Curtis, who had just taken over after the sudden death of O'Meara in late 1918, proposed a compromise of $140. This compromise the men rejected. They held out for $200 and in the end they got $200.

But therein lies the inadequacy of his account. By not explaining Coolidge's position as Coolidge himself understood it, the historian is able to criticize Coolidge without showing precisely wherein his reasoning is in error. What was needed in Professor McCoy's account of the police strike was a full and fair articulation of how Coolidge understood the issues at stake. And if Coolidge's understanding was defective, then the historian was free to state clearly where and why it was defective. In the absence of such a demonstration we remain unpersuaded that the duly constituted authorities of the State of Massachusetts were under any obligation to compromise with lawbreakers.

Central to Coolidge's stand during the police strike was his attachment to the principles of democratic government. In a democracy the rule of force or fraud is replaced by rule based upon the consent of the governed. The people make and unmake the laws. Obedience to the law cannot be used as a bargaining chip without in principle calling into question majority rule itself. In a free society illegal force, or the threat of such force, has no place. And the statesman who gives way before such threats undermines to that extent the cause of free government itself. These were the simple propositions that lay behind everything Coolidge said and did during the troubles in Boston. They are propositions that no partisan of constitutional democracy will lightly dismiss.

Professor McCoy, while admitting that Governor Coolidge backed the police commissioner, says that he did so "passively at first and later through timid action . . ." He portrays Coolidge as a man loath to get involved and slow to act when he did. ("He would be guided by public pressure and the need for stability, though none too quickly.")[25] Unfortunately, Professor McCoy once again finds himself in a disagreement with the facts.

25. McCoy, *Coolidge*, p. 86.

The truth is that Coolidge supported Curtis to the hilt from the very beginning to the very end of the entire crisis. He supported Curtis in public and he supported Curtis in private. He supported him in season and out. He supported him before, during, and after the strike.

The central and most massive fact of the Boston police strike was Coolidge's support for Commissioner Curtis. It was Coolidge's support of Curtis that brought on the strike. It was Coolidge's support of Curtis that caused the downfall of Peters. It was Coolidge's support of Curtis that sparked the deadly exchange with Gompers. And it was Coolidge's support of Curtis that occasioned the governor's proclamation of September twenty-fourth, which was the ground upon which the state campaign was fought.

Calvin Coolidge was not a bombastic or theatrical politician. He spoke softly when he spoke at all. But when he gave his word he stood by it. If there is one thing upon which his contemporaries agreed, friends and enemies alike, it was that Coolidge was a man of candor. With respect to the police strike our thesis is simple: Coolidge, not once and not ambiguously but repeatedly and unmistakeably, expressed his determination to back Curtis. And when the time came he backed him.

1. Despite the doubts of Coolidge's later critics, there was no doubt in anyone's mind at the time of the police crisis that Coolidge was behind Curtis from the earliest moment. On August 14 the *Boston Evening Transcript* reported:

> There has been no little talk, as has been said in these
> columns, about reference of the case by the policemen to
> Governor Coolidge. No such move will probably be taken at
> present, because there is a well defined opinion in the
> department that the Governor is squarely behind the police
> commissioner and will back him up in anything that he
> attempts to do, under his rights, as head of the department, to

prevent what the commissioner contends is a movement
against public policy.[26]

2. On August 17 Governor Coolidge issued a statement
to the *Transcript:*

> I am thoroughly in sympathy with the attitude of the
> commissioner as I understand it. . . I sincerely hope the
> matter will be adjusted amicably, but I have every
> confidence in the ability and judgment of Mr. Curtis and I
> intend to support him in any action he may take. Mr. Curtis
> is the police commissioner and I intend to allow him a free
> hand in the management of the department.[27]

3. On August 19 Coolidge issued the following statement
to the press:

> Mr. Curtis is the police commissioner, entrusted by law with
> the duty of conducting the office. I have no intention of
> removing him and, as long as he is commissioner, I am going
> to support him.[28]

Professor McCoy does not quote or even mention any of
the foregoing statements.

4. On August 21 the Boston Central Labor Union, which
was supporting the police, visited Governor Coolidge.

> The committee took their by now familiar position that the
> controversy was not just a police affair but concerned all
> organized labor. Coolidge listened with silent passivity, merely
> remarking afterward that he stood by his earlier statement.
> For the union leaders it was a rebuff.[29]

26. *Boston Evening Transcript*, August 14, 1919, p. 3.
27. Francis Russell, *A City in Terror* (New York: Viking Press, 1975; Penguin
    Books 1977), p. 80.
28. *Boston Evening Transcript*, August 19, 1919, p. 1.
29. Russell, *A City in Terror*, p. 88.

5. On September 4 the Commissioner had planned to pass sentence on the nineteen convicted union leaders. Mayor Peters went to Coolidge and begged him to intervene with the commissioner. Coolidge refused to intervene with Curtis.

6. On Monday, September 8, in the face of the impending strike, Curtis sent a secret emissary to Coolidge to find out what he would do if the police struck. Coolidge said:

> I am very friendly to Ned Curtis. I am told that he feels
> that enough policemen will remain loyal so that he can handle
> the situation, but you may tell him from me that if any
> emergency arises whereby it becomes necessary for me to act,
> I will stand back of him to the fullest extent.[30]

7. At dinner that night with Peters and Storrow, the governor "again refused to speak the word that would have meant compromise."[31]

8. On Tuesday, September 9, the Massachusetts branch of the AFL sent Coolidge a telegram demanding the removal of Curtis, "who has insulted organized labor." (The previous day the AFL convention at Greenfield had passed a resolution condemning "the Hunnish attitude of Police Commissioner Curtis. . .") Coolidge wired back: "In my judgment it would not be wise to remove Commissioner Curtis."[32]

9. Coolidge and Peters met again that evening. Again Coolidge refused to interfere with Curtis. Afterwards he sent the mayor a letter for the record, in which he said, among other things: "We must all support the Commissioner in the execution of the laws."[33]

30. Ibid., p. 118.
31. Ibid.
32. Ibid., p. 119.
33. Horace Green, *The Life of Calvin Coolidge* (New York: Duffield and Company, 1924), p. 130.

10. And finally, lest there be any lingering flicker of doubt that Coolidge intended to support Curtis to the fullest, we quote from the official report of the Storrow Committee itself:

> And in justice to the Governor it should be stated that at all times he assured the members of your committee that whenever called upon for a military force he would provide sufficient men—if they could be secured—to maintain law and order.[34]

On Wednesday, September 10, Mayor Peters took command of the police away from Curtis. The next day Coolidge took command of the police away from Peters and returned it to Commissioner Curtis. He had been as good as his word.[35]

Many of Coolidge's critics imply that he intervened in the actual strike in no way until it was broken. The readers of these critics are led to believe that the strike began Tuesday night, Mayor Peters called out the State Guard within Boston on Wednesday, the strike was broken by Thursday morning, and then Coolidge needlessly took command and called out the entire State Guard on Thursday afternoon.

The actual sequence of events was as follows: The strike began on Tuesday evening. In the early morning hours on Wednesday violence occurred. On Wednesday morning Coolidge sent a message to Mayor Peters that he was awaiting any request Peters might want to make of him. But Peters had already called out the State Guard within Boston (about one thousand men) and had sent Coolidge a request for three thousand more troops to report at 5:00 P.M. Coolidge promptly called out nearly the entire State

34. *The Boston Police Strike: Two Reports*, "Report of the Citizen's Committee," p. 14.
35. McCoy, *Coolidge*, p. 86.

Guard to report immediately. Within hours guardsmen were pouring into Boston from all parts of Massachusetts. By Thursday morning there were nearly five thousand troops in the streets of Boston. These troops, called out by Peters and Coolidge, were sufficient to restore order.

We do not believe that either the governor or the mayor deserves any special commendation for these acts. They did their simple duty. But neither do we believe that the facts ought to be distorted to make it appear as if they did any less than their duty.

Some people have wondered why either Peters or Coolidge did not call out the Guard the moment the police walked off their jobs. In fact the two men have been accused of passing the decision to call out the troops back and forth like a hot potato. But both had good reasons for not acting hastily. In his *Autobiography* Coolidge explains his reasons:

> I have always felt that I should have called out the State
> Guard as soon as the police left their posts. The
> Commissioner did not feel this was necessary. The Mayor,
> who was a man of high character, and a personal friend, but
> of the opposite party, had conferred with me. He had the
> same authority as the Governor to call out all the Guard in
> the City of Boston. It would be very unusual for a Governor to
> act except on the request of the local authorities. No
> disorder existed, and it would have been rather a violent
> assumption that it was threatened, but it could have been
> made.[36]

We cannot help but agree, even in retrospect, that for the governor to have called out the Guard, not only without a request from the mayor but against the recommendation of the commissioner, and at a moment when public order was not threatened, would indeed have been "very

36. Coolidge, *Autobiography*, pp. 130-131.

unusual." And yet the mayor had every reason not to rush
out the Guard precipitously. Curtis and Coolidge were
Republicans, Peters a Democrat. The police were Boston
Irish. Peters was at every point in favor of a peaceful,
compromise solution of the conflict between the commissioner and his men. No doubt he reasoned that if Curtis
and Coolidge wished to be intransigent, they should act as
their own enforcers. They should take the responsibility for
their own decision.

The question of who should have called out the troops is
in our judgment immaterial. Both Coolidge and Peters
stood ready to act if action was called for. Both had good
reasons, in law and prudence, for holding back. When
violence broke out both acted promptly and manfully. We
concur with the verdict of Horace Green:

> . . . it must be remembered that there was no appreciable
> rioting until eleven p.m., September 9th, 1919. Thereupon
> and thereafter all parties concerned acted with all speed
> permitted by statutory technicalities. We who judge do so
> from the point of view of spectators after the event.[37]

The more important half of this phase of the strike is not
the military but the political. It would have been a serious
political error to commit the troops early on. Coolidge
recognized this:

> Such action probably would have saved some property, but
> would have decided no issue. In fact it would have made it
> more difficult to maintain the position Mr. Curtis had taken,
> and which I was supporting, because the issue was not
> understood, and the disorder focused public attention on it,
> and showed just what it meant to have a police force that
> did not obey orders.[38]

37. Green, *Life of Coolidge*, pp. 147-148.
38. Coolidge, *Autobiography*, p. 131.

Sometimes in politics the essence of prudence is not to go over to the offensive prematurely. Lincoln recognized this at the time of Fort Sumter. In the words of one historian, he seemed "lost in indecision." "My policy," said Lincoln, "is to have no policy." But there are times, as shrewd politicians know, when seeming to have no policy is the very best policy of all.[39]

In retrospect, it is clear that the need for additional military action had passed by Thursday noon. Virtually the entire State Guard was on patrol. The strike was broken. At the time, however, this was not clear, because the threat of a general strike remained. Coolidge busied himself with many preparations, including the creation of a vast citizen militia to fight any general strike, and a request that federal troops be held in readiness. There can be no question but that Coolidge would have been just as hard-nosed during a protracted strike as he had been when he slammed thousands of troops into Boston on Wednesday and as he had been during the weeks leading up to the strike.

The *political* aspect of the strike, however, was not resolved by Thursday noon. It was the intention of Mayor Peters, now that he had seized the initiative, to work out a compromise settlement along the lines proposed by the Storrow Committee. We take up again McCoy's narrative from midday Wednesday through noon on Thursday.

> Pressures in the meantime mounted on Coolidge to intervene. Commissioner Curtis went to him in great distress. Both the commissioner and the governor were worried that the issue that had precipitated the strike would be lost. They feared that Mayor Peters, now that he was in command, would submit the police strikers' grievances to arbitration.

39. "While Storrow declared that he personally would doubtless have had the troops ready, he admitted that Abraham Lincoln would probably have met the emergency as Coolidge did." Fuess, *Coolidge*, p. 230.

That was unlikely as the mayor did not have the Storrow
Committee's support. Yet no one knew or could predict what
Peters might do under stress. Governor Coolidge did not
care to find out. As he put it in his autobiography:
  "I did not see how it was possible to arbitrate the
question of the authority of the law, or of the necessity of
obedience to the rules of the Department and the orders of
the commissioner. These principles were the heart of the
whole controversy and the only important questions at
issue. It can readily be seen how important they were and
what the effect might have been if they had not been
maintained. I decided to support them whatever the
consequences might be. I fully expected it would result in
my defeat in the coming campaign for reelection as governor."
  Yet Coolidge waited through another night of troubles
before standing on his principles.[40]

It is fascinating sometimes to see how a historian orders
his material. The quotation from Coolidge, a more extensive version of which we reproduced earlier, in its original
context referred to the events leading up to the strike. Yet
McCoy did not reproduce the quotation in his narrative of
the events at the appropriate point. Had he done so Coolidge's conduct would have appeared more plausible. The
insertion of the quotation at this point allows McCoy to
juxtapose the last sentence of the quotation ("I fully expected
it would result in my defeat in the coming campaign . . .")
with the first sentence of McCoy's commentary ("Yet Coolidge waited through another night of troubles before standing on his principles.") in such a way as to suggest that
Coolidge's bold words were belied by his dilatory actions.
  This is simply untrue. When Commissioner Curtis came
to Coolidge in distress on Wednesday afternoon the governor assured him *at that time* of his support.[41] Anything else
would have been totally inconsistent with everything Coo-

40. McCoy, *Coolidge*, pp. 90-91.
41. Russell, *City of Terror*, p. 150.

lidge had said and done until that moment. We repeat what we have said several times: the most prominent thread running through the governor's conduct before, during, and after the strike was support for Curtis:

> It was soon reported to me that the Mayor, acting under a special law, had taken charge of the police force of the city, and by putting a Guard officer in command had virtually displaced the Commissioner, who came to me in great distress. If he was to be superseded I thought the men that he had discharged might be taken back and the cause lost. Certainly they and the rest of the policemen's union must have rejoiced at his discomfort. . . . The strike occurred Tuesday night, the Guard were called Wednesday, and Thursday I issued a General Order restoring Mr. Curtis to his place as Commissioner in control of the police, and made a proclamation calling on all citizens to assist me in preserving order, and especially directing all police officers in Boston to obey the orders of Mr. Curtis.
>
> This was the important contribution I made to the tactics of the situation, which has never been fully realized.[42]

It is of no importance that Coolidge waited overnight to reinstate the commissioner. If McCoy is right in thinking that it was "unlikely" that Peters would act at all, then it is a thousand times more unlikely that Peters would have made any conciliatory gestures toward the policemen at the height of the street fighting! (Which, as we know, he did not.) It is true, however, that Peters, in a midday meeting on Thursday with leaders of the Boston Central Labor Union, suggested to them that a settlement could be reached. Shortly thereafter Governor Coolidge coldly cut him down.

In the days and weeks following the strike Curtis and Coolidge were as uncompromising as they had been from the start. They said that they were opposed to reinstate-

42. Coolidge, *Autobiography*, pp. 131-133.

ment of any of the striking policemen, and they meant it. Not one of the striking policemen ever again worked for the Boston police force.

It has been said that actions speak louder than words and that the pen is mightier than the sword. Some students of politics have believed that the pen can be dispensed with altogether; others would cast aside the sword. Both misunderstand the human soul.

Sound statesmanship is necessarily a blend of speech and deed. Noble speech without the corresponding deed must be hollow or hypocritical. But deed without speech remains unjustified and deed unjustified must in the end be undone.

Many who have written about the police strike discuss Coolidge's rhetoric as a kind of an afterthought. Just as they attribute the timing of Coolidge's actions to luck, so they also seem to believe that Samuel Gompers was hit with a lucky rhetorical shot. In our conclusion we intend to say a few words about Coolidge's timing and tactics. Here we wish to say a brief word about his rhetoric.

It is a mistake made by many who write about the strike nowadays to suggest that Coolidge became a national hero because he was thought to have taken firm action to break the strike. Certainly this was a factor, but the public and Coolidge's admirers in the media regarded it as secondary. They believed that his firm military stand was subordinate to his firm moral stand. "Coolidge's primary contribution," said Horace Green, "was to focus the sentiment first of the state, then of the nation, on the issues involved, and, with the crystallization of public opinion, to press them in a never-to-be-forgotten way."[43] Green knew perfectly well that Mayor Peters deserved as much credit at least as Coolidge for mobilizing the Guard, but mobilizing the

43. Green, *Life of Coolidge,* p. 123.

Guard was infinitely less important than mobilizing public opinion.

> It is not to be denied that others would have stepped in more promptly. It is not to be denied that Coolidge moved along behind the interference, as was his constitutional right. It is true that B'rer Rabbit stayed outside the briar patch while the lesser animals got tangled up. But when the time came, B'rer Rabbit said something mighty cute. And all the other animals clapped their hands and said, "That's just what I've been thinking."[44]

Coolidge's celebrated telegram to Samuel Gompers, which was carefully crafted and sent to the newspapers in time for their early Monday morning editions, was the centerpiece in a whole series of public utterances by Coolidge during the strike. In all of them he displayed compelling vigor and clarity. His proclamations on Thursday, September eleventh, in which he took command of the situation; his press interview the following day; his telegram to Gompers; his proclamation of September twenty-fourth denouncing talk of reinstatement of the strikers; and his various campaign addresses all mark him as a politician who could use words to great effect.

This is not to say that Coolidge was a great orator. He was not. (It was said when Coolidge was Lieutenant Governor that Governor McCall could fill any hall in Massachusetts and Coolidge could empty it!) But he was, as we have had occasion to remark previously, as fine a writer of English prose as any president in this century. And we must remember that the vast majority of citizens who were stirred by his telegram to Gompers and by his interviews, speeches, and proclamations, *read* them in the newspapers.

44. Ibid., pp. 124-125.

We cannot regard this as mere happenstance. Again and again throughout his political career Coolidge caught the imagination of the public on important occasions. Upon being elected President of the Massachusetts State Senate, he delivered what McCoy believes to be the finest speech of his life. ("Have Faith in Massachusetts") His first State of the Union Address and his Inaugural Address were received with great enthusiasm across the country. Recent research has shown that he was most effective as a radio speaker during the 1924 campaign.

Quite apart from his effect upon his constituents, Coolidge in many of his speeches achieved a level of thoughtfulness that is rare among politicians. His speeches on education and the liberal arts are little gems. His Lincoln Day speech in 1924 is one of the most commonsensical and persuasive speeches ever delivered by an American president on the subject of fiscal policy. His beautiful Fourth of July speeches (especially those of 1916 and 1926) show him to be a close student and follower of Abraham Lincoln within the tradition of American politics. None of these, of course, has ever come near to getting into the history books. But we believe that anyone who reads them will recognize in their author a man who could think and write clearly and movingly, and whose hold over his contemporaries was not merely fortuitous.

Professor McCoy, as we have noted, makes three criticisms of Governor Coolidge's handling of the police strike. The evidence at our disposal has compelled us to disagree with those criticisms.

1. We do not believe that Commissioner Curtis is censurable for his opposition to affiliation with the AFL. His position on that issue is indistinguishable from that of Storrow and Peters. Nor do we believe him to be censurable for refusing to waive sentence on the nineteen convicted policemen, in the face of a strike threat, any more

than a judge is censurable for sentencing premeditated and unrepentant lawbreakers in the face of a threat by their accomplices to burn down the courthouse. Under the circumstances we cannot indict Coolidge for backing Curtis in the stand he took.

2. We believe that only a total blackout of the historical record allowed McCoy to pretend that Coolidge's support of Curtis was anything but unequivocal.

3. We do not believe that the mere fact that Coolidge waited until Thursday to reinstate Commissioner Curtis is proof of his timidity.

Says McCoy: ". . . prominence came to Coolidge largely from the strike, an affair in which he did little and from which he deserved little." We say: The Boston police strike is a textbook case of Coolidge's modus operandi, and reveals unmistakeably his ability to play the lion and the fox. If one believes the former interpretation one sees the strike as a political shootout in which one by one the gunfighters fall down dead or wounded and in the end Coolidge stands atop the heap of bodies and *it was all luck!* Storrow is brushed aside, Curtis is discredited, Peters is cut down, Gompers is silenced, the policemen lose their jobs, Long is crushed, and Coolidge, who did nothing, goes on to the presidency!

The key to the political success of Calvin Coolidge may be found in the phrase "economy of force." He always accumulated political influence and power slowly and carefully and behind the scenes. After he had calculated a given situation to his satisfaction he would act swiftly and decisively and with sufficient resources to achieve his goal.

> A second conclusion with which those who have studied Coolidge's mental habits will agree, is that before, during, and after the strike, he behaved altogether as we should expect of him. We have by this time learned, as Frank W. Stearns learned long ago, that throughout Coolidge's career,

patience of investigation, seeming indecision while
studying the winds, but speed of action when his mind was
made up, are fundamental traits.[46]

At one point or another every figure in the police strike
attempted to seize the initiative *without having the power
to do so*. The reason they did not have the power was that
Coolidge held all of the ultimate legal, military, and political power in his hands. It is not surprising, therefore, that
in the end he prevailed and they did not. Coolidge's political task was to avoid taking the initiative too early, appear
to react to events, and await his opportunities. The only
hope that his opponents had was that he would lack moral
power. But he was a rock, and against him they could not
prevail.

The police were the first to misplay their hand. In the
first instance they misjudged the commissioner and in the
second they miscalculated their support among labor and
the public for a strike. If they had waited and had voted to
accept the Storrow compromise, then Curtis would have
borne the entire brunt of public disapproval; the police
could have remained in the role of underdogs. But they
were, so to speak, too stiff-necked.

The Storrow Committee attempted to bring about a
settlement but was powerless and therefore irrelevant.

Commissioner Curtis was mistaken in his assurances to
Coolidge and Peters that he had the situation under control. Coolidge, of course, did not take him completely at
his word, and was—again behind the scenes—readying
the State Guard. When it became clear that Curtis's assurance that he could protect the city was hollow, Coolidge
sent the entire Guard into Boston.

Mayor Peters made a bold but foolish lunge for power,
but Coolidge easily pushed him aside, assumed control of

45. Green, *Life of Coolidge*, p. 124.

the situation himself, and restored command of the police to Curtis.

Gompers, in the face of an aroused public opinion, took entirely the wrong tone in his communication to Coolidge, and left himself wide open to the rebuke he received.

Coolidge, by contrast, at each point did what he had to do without overreaching himself. He was determined to support Curtis but he did so without seeming to become the aggressor against labor. He was determined to protect Boston but he did so without appearing heavy-handed. He was determined that the issues at stake should not be lost and so he removed Peters from control. He was determined that the issues at stake should not be misunderstood and so he stated them plainly and forcefully.

Coolidge's initial decision to back Curtis, from which all the other events flowed with a kind of inevitability, was not an accident; it was a policy. His refusal to compromise was not an accident; his willingness to send troops, to raise a militia, to request federal intervention were not accidents; his opposition to reinstatement was no accident; his powers of expression were no accident.

What some people call luck or accident, we would call opportunity. An opportunity came to Calvin Coolidge, without which, it is true, he may never have become president. What the Great Depression was to Franklin Roosevelt the police strike was to Calvin Coolidge. It brought him to center stage. It shone the national spotlight upon him. It provided a public test of his character and his intellect. It revealed him for what he was. And the American people approved of what they saw.

Three

McNary-Haugen

The McNary-Haugen farm relief legislation was the bone of contention in the greatest congressional dogfight of the 1920s. The fight began in January 1924 with the introduction in Congress of the first McNary-Haugen bill. For several years neither that bill nor any of its legislative descendants could command a majority in either house of Congress. McNary-Haugen bills finally were passed in 1927 and again in 1928, but President Coolidge vetoed both of them.

The story of McNary-Haugen, in the conventional telling, is a classic illustration of the two themes that dominate nearly all political histories of the 1920s: first, that the Republican presidents of the twenties were spokesmen for business interests, as over against the interests of other groups in society; and second, that they espoused a creed —whether of laissez-faire capitalism or of rugged individualism—that was inappropriate to the times.

In the story of McNary-Haugen, as told by our leading historians, President Coolidge, the representative of big business, turned a deaf ear to the cries of America's distressed farmers, who were suffering through a prolonged depression.

It was well known that Coolidge held no brief for new or unconventional ideas. The "business of the United States is business," he had said. In a vague way this meant that business should be positively assisted by high tariffs and, in

some cases, by outright government subsidies, as well as by
reduced taxes and a minimum of government regulation or
interference. He positively opposed any government aid or
support to agriculture and labor. . . . The President
emphatically stated his position on agricultural problems in his
first annual message. . . . Senator Pat Harrison wryly
remarked that the section of the President's message he liked
the best was where he told the farmers to go to hell![1]

1. Gilbert Fite, *George N. Peek and the Fight for Farm Parity* (Norman:
University of Oklahoma Press, 1954), pp. 77-78. We have remarked
earlier that the one-eyed view of the twenties so prevalent among historians has the unfortunate effect of inculcating a dogmatic attitude toward the
period in the minds of students. Students are rarely offered any serious or
sophisticated account of the policies of men like President Coolidge. They
are offered instead stereotypes or caricatures. The arguments in the above
passage from the historian Gilbert Fite are a caricature of arguments that
we will attempt to discuss seriously in chapter 3. For the moment we note
the following: (1) Coolidge did hold to two ideas, production control and
cooperative farming, that were for all practical purposes "new," and that
were also "unconventional," if we mean by unconventional not "conform-
ing to established practice," which is what the dictionary means by it. (2)
Coolidge did not say that the "business of the United States is business."
This is a misquotation. (3) If the historian had bothered to look up the exact
words to the quotation, he certainly would have noticed that in context it
has nothing to do, not even "vaguely," with tariffs, taxes, or government
regulation. (4) Fites says that Coolidge believed that business should be
"positively assisted" by government but that in the case of agriculture he
"positively opposed" any government aid. The positive assistance mentioned with respect to business consisted of high tariffs, tax reduction, and
a minimum of government interference. Yet Fite himself mentions elsewhere that Coolidge favored high tariffs, tax reduction, and a minimum of
government interference for agriculture as well! (Coolidge himself pointed
out that farmers had the advantage of corporations in the matter of taxation
because the individual tax rate was much lower than the corporate tax rate.
With respect to government regulation he noted that farm coops were
effectively exempted from the anti-trust laws. With respect to the tariff he
made the argument that everything bought by the farmer qua farmer was
on the duty-free list.) We know of no direct government subsidy to
business that did not have its origin and its justification in the war years.
We do know, however, that the government under Coolidge promoted
directly internal improvements in order to lower transportation costs for
farmers and that it attempted in effect to subsidize the promotion of
fertilizer at Muscle Shoals for the benefit of Southern agriculture. The
former, of course, was long-standing Republican policy; the latter had its
origin and justification in the war years.

According to his academic critics, President Coolidge's public justification for his opposition to farm relief was his dedication to laissez-faire principles. On February 25, 1927, Coolidge sent his first McNary-Haugen veto message to Congress: "The entire discourse was a promulgation of the laissez-faire position for agriculture."[2] On May 23, 1928, the president sent his second McNary-Haugen veto message to Congress: "The author, in place of analyzing the measure carefully, let play upon its essential principles the full force of his fundamentally laissez-faire reactions."[3] "His real objection was a stubborn determination to do nothing . . . a doctrinaire unwillingness to depart from laissez-faire."[4]

But Coolidge, the champion of laissez-faire for agriculture, was at the same time the champion of high tariffs for business: "In 1927 . . . the McNary-Haugen bill passed both houses of Congress. Coolidge—on the same day that he issued a proclamation increasing the tariff on pig iron 50 per cent—vetoed the bill in an unwontedly wrathful message."[5] He was, that is to say, a hypocrite, whether conscious or unconscious.

It would not be correct to infer from the well-nigh universal condemnation by historians of Coolidge's opposition to McNary-Haugen that these historians themselves favor the legislation. On the contrary, most of them concede that Coolidge directed some telling blows against it. In fact the consensus among historians is that the bill was simply unworkable.

The gravamen of the indictment against Coolidge is that

---

2. Ibid., p. 179.
3. John Black, "The McNary-Haugen Movement," *American Economic Review*, September 1928, p. 412.
4. Rexford G. Tugwell, "Reflections on Farm Relief," *Political Science Quarterly*, December 1928, p. 487.
5. Schlesinger, *Crisis*, p. 109.

he was officially indifferent to the plight of the farmers. Because of his pro-business sympathies or his laissez-faire sentiments, or both, he refused to do anything for them. This do-nothing attitude is frequently contrasted with the can-do spirit of Franklin Roosevelt and the New Deal. Historians generally admit that FDR was not a profound student of economics, but they praise his economic pragmatism. At least, they say, he was willing to try things, to experiment. He was open to new ideas. Moreover, Roosevelt, as a committed social and economic democrat, was an advocate of social and economic justice.

FDR, in contrast to his Republican predecessors, was the model statesman. His attachment to the common good led him to see the simple justice in the farmers' demands for "equality for agriculture." His pragmatism freed him from the shibboleths of laissez-faire capitalism and left him open to the advanced and unpopular ideas of various intellectuals and academic students of the agricultural question. And Roosevelt was frankly willing to use the power of the federal government to implement those ideas.

Of course Roosevelt knew perfectly well that power, unless it is responsible power, is dangerous. But the mating of new ideas and power (the Harvard-Washington axis) would be supervised by the pragmatic statesman subject to the approval of the people themselves. The responsible exercise of power is the middle way between the abdication of power on the one hand and the exercise of total power on the other, just as pragmatism is the middle way between the ideological extremes of left and right.

President Roosevelt was an activist; he was pragmatic and open; he was a democrat. President Coolidge was none of the above. President Roosevelt was determined to do all he could to help the farmers, and he succeeded. President Coolidge was determined to do nothing to help the farmers, and he succeeded, too. This is what students of American history read in their history books.

We turn now to one of those history books, in accordance with our approach in chapters 1 and 2. In Chapter 13 of *The Crisis of the Old·Order* ("Protest on the Countryside") Professor Schlesinger extends his critique of the Republican administrations of the twenties to their agricultural policies. We have seen already that Professor Schlesinger regards conservatives in general and the Republican Party in particular as handmaidens of the plutocracy. As he wrote long ago in the *Nation,*

> . . . since the disappearance of Federalism American conservatives have been characteristically concerned with quick, short-term advantages for themselves and not with the interests of the nation or the welfare of society. A recurrent casualty of the American political culture has been the conservative with high ideals of social responsibility trapped in a plutocratic and short-sighted party.[6]

Seen through the eyes of Professor Schlesinger the 1920s were one long stampede by business to make money, a stampede blessed by that apostle of acquisitiveness, Calvin Coolidge, who was subservient to big business but indifferent toward labor and farmers. Against this background Professor Schlesinger begins his thematic chapter on agriculture:

> The American farmers had risen nobly to the challenge of war. In the decade after 1910, they had increased the aggregate acreage harvested by nearly 15 percent. American food saved much of Europe from hunger and revolution.[7]

Mr. Schlesinger had begun his previous chapter with a sketch of the old Wilsonians watching the "ignoble motives" of the New Era. He begins the present chapter with a sketch of the nobility of the farmers. In our opinion this

6. Arthur Schlesinger, *Nation*, March 13, 1948, p. 306.
7. Schlesinger, *Crisis*, p. 105.

way of writing has about as much relation to real history as
a Harlequin Romance has to real literature. We do not
wish to denigrate the patriotism of America's farmers. It is
as genuine as any other man's. But it is *also* true that the
farmers griped incessantly during World War I and com-
plained frequently that they were not getting enough money.
The tremendous speculative boom in agriculture during
and after the war was ignited by that well known explosive
combination of patriotism *and* profit. Whether that boom
might properly be described as a stampede to make money
is not a question dealt with by Mr. Schlesinger at this
point. But he does note that prosperity was followed by
privation:

> While businessmen in the cities marvelled at having solved
> the secret of prosperity, the farmers, in gloom and indignation,
> watched gross agricultural income fall from $17.7 billion in
> 1919 to $10.5 billion in 1921.[8]

How businessmen in the cities in 1921 could have been
marvelling at having solved the secret of prosperity, when
in fact corporate profits were taking a shocking plunge, is
not explained by our historian. In 1919 corporate profits,
after taxes, were $6.241 billion. In 1921 they were minus $
.243 billion.

It is, however, true that as time went on agriculture
recovered more slowly from the depression than did the
rest of the economy. Mr. Schlesinger summarizes the problems of the farmers and then comes to their proposed
solution:

> As early as 1921, agricultural senators and representatives
> began to huddle together in the so-called Farm Bloc.
>   "Under the policy of protection we have built up a great

8. Ibid.

industrial nation," said Senator Capper of Kansas in 1922, "and the same protection cannot now be withheld from agriculture if we would preserve the balance between industrial and agricultural growth."

But the problem remained to work out this protective principle in legislation.[9]

Schlesinger then goes on to describe the genesis of the McNary-Haugen plan, which, when it finally reached President Coolidge's desk years later, was vetoed "on the same day that he issued a proclamation increasing the tariff on pig iron 50 per cent." This is an astonishing passage but it is vintage Schlesinger. The student who comes upon this passage will come away with the impression that President Coolidge favored the protective principle for industry but was against it for agriculture. He will quite naturally therefore be filled with indignation against the favoritism of Coolidge—as we were when we first read this passage many years ago. But Professor Schlesinger achieves this effect—like a good conjurer—through misdirection: what his audience does *not* see is as important as what it does.

1. He mentions McNary-Haugen, which in 1922 was an embryo, but he does *not* mention the Emergency Tariff Act of 1921, "which," as Senator Capper himself said, "was primarily designed to protect agriculture . . ."

2. He does *not* mention the Fordney-McCumber Tariff of 1922 in which we find the agricultural rates carried over from the emergency tariff.

3. So far as we have been able to discover, there is no mention in the first hundred pages of Schlesinger's book of the existence of an agricultural tariff. (cf. p.64: "So Coolidge similarly cherished the high wall of protection *for American industry* erected in the Republican tariff of 1922."—Italics mine.)

9. Ibid., pp. 105-106.

4. Schlesinger quotes Senator Capper on the need for
protection for agriculture, but he gives no hint that the
Harding Administration had attempted to meet that need.
Since the professor is so fond of quoting Senator Capper
(he quotes him again less than a page later), we wonder
why he did not refer his readers to page 143 of Capper's
book, where the senator in summing up the accomplish-
ments of Congress with respect to agriculture during the
first session of the Harding Administration, mentions first,
"The Emergency Tariff," and second, "The Fordney Tariff
Bill."[10]

We have seen to this point that Professor Schlesinger
makes very effective use of omission. By omitting any
discussion of the farmers' baser motives during the war
boom, by omitting to mention that American business lost
a quarter of a billion dollars in 1921, and by omitting any
acknowledgment of the existence of an agricultural tariff,
Professor Schlesinger creates a certain kind of world for his
reader, a world in which the Good Guys (farmers) are in
mortal conflict with the Bad Guys (big business and the
Republicans). Lest any reader—impervious to the charms
of subtlety—still have the good guys and the bad guys
confused, Schlesinger now sorts them out definitively:

> . . . in Henry C. Wallace, Harding's Secretary of
> Agriculture, Peek found a sympathetic listener.
>   Wallace, who had been for many years editor of *Wallace's
> Farmer*, knew the worries of the grain belt. *But he discovered
> himself almost alone in his concern in the Harding
> Administration*. "The farmers of America," reported Senator
> Capper bitterly in 1922, "found themselves being opposed
> instead of aided, by business groups which should be the best
> friends of agriculture." The appointed voice of business in
> the cabinet was, of course, Secretary Hoover; and Hoover had

10. Arthur Capper, *The Agricultural Bloc* (New York: Harcourt Brace and
Company, 1922), p. 143.

ideas of his own about what he persisted in calling "the
agricultural industry." In 1920 the Washington representative
of the Grange had pronounced him, of all the presidential
possibilities, "the most objectionable to the farmers of this
country." "His dealings with hog and milk and beef
producers," said Wallace the same year in reference to the
War Food Administration, "gave evidence of a mental bias
which causes farmers to thoroughly distrust him. They look
upon him as an autocrat of big business."[11] (Italics mine.)

And a few sentences later:

> Wallace . . . tried to strengthen the Department, particularly
> by organizing the Bureau of Agricultural Economics; but his
> effort to gain a voice for agriculture in the business
> administration was an uphill job. "Unless farmers as a
> class get busy and *fight* for their rights," he told
> an advisor, "we in the Department will not long be
> able to take a national point of view because the
> point of view of other interests will dominate us."[12]

To this point in the chapter Schlesinger has quoted
Senator Capper twice, Secretary Wallace twice (once attacking Hoover directly) and the head of the Grange once
(attacking Hoover). It goes without saying that Hoover is
not permitted to speak even a single sentence in his own
defense. ("Our taste today is more fastidious . . . our
partialities more contained . . .") But Mr. Schlesinger is
not content merely to discuss the issues. After describing
briefly the political battle in Washington over the McNary-
Haugen bill in 1924, he concludes as follows:

> The Secretary's energy, though, was beginning to ebb.
> Worn by Hoover's incessant opposition, racked by sciatica,
> Wallace labored beyond his strength in the McNary-Haugen
> fight and on a book of his own about the farm crisis. In

11. Schlesinger, *Crisis*, pp. 106-107.
12. Ibid., p. 107.

> October he went to the hospital for an operation. A week later
> he was dead. "Many said that the situation in Washington
> killed Wallace," wrote a close associate. "Others made it more
> definite and personal." Coolidge promptly offered the vacant
> Agricultural job to Hoover. Hoover turned it down; the post
> went instead to W. M. Jardine, who admired the Commerce
> Department and, as Hoover laconically wrote, "established at
> once full cooperation with us."[13]

Our historian in the first instance apparently gives equal
weight to Hoover's opposition and the sciatica as causes for
Wallace's ebbing strength, his admission to the hospital,
and his subsequent death. But he is not content to leave
the impression of equality. He proceeds, with no further
reference to the sciatica: "Many said the situation in Washington killed Wallace. . . . Others made it more definite
and personal."

What can be said of an historian who repeats without
contradiction a terrible charge, uttered in great bitterness
and grief during an intensely partisan dispute? What need
was there to weave Hoover into what could have been a
straightforward account of Wallace's untimely end? For
such an account one has only to turn to the standard
biographies of Wallace.

The fact is that Wallace's strength did not ebb because
he was "worn by Hoover's incessant opposition." The
McNary-Haugen bill had already been defeated in the
House of Representatives on June third. Wallace did not
enter the hospital until October. ("Worn by the incessant
opposition of the House of Representatives, racked by
sciatica . . .") During the summer of 1924, while working
on his book, Wallace was suffering severe attacks of sciatica. But even rest from his labors did not relieve the pain
because his illness, in fact, was due to an infected gall
bladder, which itself was probably the result of an attack of

13. Ibid., pp. 107-108.

typhoid fever that he had sustained more than twenty years before. Wallace died from complications that developed after the surgical removal of the gall bladder. It is true that the Wallace family was bitter against Hoover. But even the younger Wallace later admitted that the bitterness was misplaced.

> "Do you know," he said slowly, "I hope I never again feel as intensely antagonistic toward anyone as I did then. . . . I felt, almost, as if Hoover had killed my father." . . .
> "That was nonsense. A fight for ideas would never hurt or kill my father. He loved to fight for ideas; he lived for it! . . . He had a bad case of typhoid when he was a teacher back at Ames . . ."[14]

One wishes that our historian had been as forthright and as charitable as was Henry A. Wallace. But apparently such is not the stuff of which prize winning history is made.

Let us return from this unseemly diversion to Schlesinger's more substantive remarks about the agricultural issue. In an earlier paragraph Mr. Schlesinger depicted the indifference of the "business administration" of Harding to the problems of agriculture. Contrary to appearances, *none* of the evidence artfully employed by Mr. Schlesinger in this paragraph is supportive of its thematic sentence. ("Wallace . . . discovered himself almost alone in his concern in the Harding Administration.") On the contrary, a careful reading of Schlesinger's own evidence reveals it to be not an indictment of the Harding Administration, but rather a damning indictment of the *Wilson* Administration.

As everyone knows, except those who have learned their American history from Mr. Schlesinger, it was the Wilson Administration that bore the brunt of the farm belt's anger

---

14. Russell Lord, *The Wallaces of Iowa* (Boston: Houghton Mifflin Company, 1947), p. 285.

at the postwar agricultural depression. The Democratic national ticket was utterly crushed throughout the Midwest in the election of 1920, and Woodrow Wilson did not redeem the popularity of his party by vetoing the emergency farm tariff shortly before he left office. This is not to say anything about the merits of Wilson's agricultural policies or about the merits of the tariff. We merely wish to remind the serious student of American politics that no administration, Republican or Democratic, has in the past fifty years been immune to the farmers' discontent.

None of this is apparent from Mr. Schlesinger's narrative. Following his thematic sentence about the lack of concern within the Harding Administration for the worries of the farm belt, Schlesinger quotes the "bitter" words of Senator Capper. Because Schlesinger gives us the date of the quotation—1922, the second year of the Harding Administration—and because the quotation is sandwiched between references to the Harding Administration, the reader naturally assumes that Capper is attacking the administration. *But this is not the case.* The senator's "bitter" words had nothing whatsoever to do with Harding. He was decrying opposition to cooperative marketing and to control of the packing industry. But these bills were passed during the Harding Administration and had the support of Harding and Hoover both. Speaking directly to the first year of the Harding Administration, Senator Capper said:

> In reviewing the accomplishments of the session in August at its close, the Republican leader in the House pointed out that few Congresses in American history had made a better record of progress through the hot summer than this, the opening session of the new administration. In the long list of measures that had been passed, there were represented more measures of interest to agriculture than are to be found in the action of any similar session in recent years.[15]

15. Capper, *Bloc,* p. 143.

And three pages later:

> From the very first meeting the Agricultural Bloc was
> favored with the constructive advice of leaders who were
> familiar with the agricultural situation . . .
>   In this group must be named Secretary of Agriculture
> Wallace, Secretary of Commerce Hoover . . .[16]

So much for the "bitter" words of Senator Capper. Professor Schlesinger continues: "In 1920 the Washington representative of the Grange had pronounced him [Hoover], of all the presidential possibilities, 'the most objectionable to the farmers of this country.'" Of course, 1920 was prior to Harding's presidency. Hoover was indeed unpopular with some farmers (although Professor Koerselman says that "most of the prominent agricultural voices" supported his nomination for Secretary of Commerce, and one of the most enthusiastic voices belonged to Senator Arthur Capper), but his unpopularity resulted from his identification with the policies of the Democratic administration of Woodrow Wilson.

> To such a correspondent complaining of the Wallace "grouch"
> against the "Hooveresque Democrats," Harry Wallace
> replied: "Guilty! No one in a position of authority with this
> administration [Wilson's] seems to have any use for the
> farmer . . ."[17]

Furthermore, most historians now concede that the criticism by farmers of Hoover's service in the War Food Administration was not fully justified—if it was justified at all—because it was based upon inadequate knowledge of

16. Ibid., p. 146. ". . . the burst of farm legislation in the early twenties has probably been surpassed only in the period of the early New Deal." Grant McConnell, 1953.
17. Lord, *The Wallaces*, p. 215.

the political pressures under which Hoover was operating.[18]

After Arthur Capper is allowed to have his full say, and after Hoover's unpopularity is traced to the Wilson Administration, and after the list of agricultural bills signed by President Harding is allowed into the record, it no longer is possible to cling to the rather crude characterization of the Harding Administration set forth in the pages of *The Crisis of the Old Order*. At that point one is obliged to look at the political situation in its complexities, its shades of gray; the real political world is rarely as clear cut as it appears in the black and white fantasies of ideologues and partisan historians. For example, the alert reader will have detected an internal dissonance in Mr. Schlesinger's attempt to portray American agriculture as lying prostrate under the heel of big business during the New Era: ". . . in 1924 an alliance between the *agricultural South* and the business community defeated the bill in the House."[19] (Emphasis mine.)

The fact is that during the 1920s many farmers, especially those in the South and East, were not prostrate but prosperous. Thus when Mr. Schlesinger advances one of his easy generalizations about class conflict in America (e.g., "The nearly eleven million Americans engaged in agriculture in 1920 were not the only group outside the orbit of the business classes.")[20] one must resist being carried away by the flow of the rhetoric. The inital vote against McNary-Haugen was essentially a *sectional*, not a class, vote. Mid-western and Western congressmen were defeated by a coalition of Southern Democratic congress-

18. Ibid., p. 213; Edward Schapsmeier and Frederick Schapsmeier, *Henry A. Wallace of Iowa: The Agrarian Years, 1910-1940* (Ames: The Iowa State University Press, 1968), p. 42.
19. Schlesinger, *Crisis*, p. 107.
20. Ibid., p. 111.

men and Eastern congressmen. The former were supported by bankers and businessmen whose fortunes were tied to those of the farmers; the latter included both representatives of agricultural and urban districts, including some progressives who voted to protect working families and consumers among their constituents from higher food prices. Until 1927 it was less the administration's opposition to McNary-Haugen that doomed the bill than it was a split in the ranks of the farmers themselves. After 1927 Coolidge's vetoes prevented the measure from becoming law. But by 1927, as Schlesinger himself concedes, the feasibility of McNary-Haugen was substantially diminished. ("Young Henry Wallace and others agreed . . . that the rise of economic nationalism was rendering both McNary-Haugen and the export debenture plan obsolete.")[21]

We do not propose to recapitulate the years of detailed debate over McNary-Haugen. Others have done so before us. We do, however, wish to comment upon the major issues in that debate. When we debate the merits of any proposal we discuss the correctness of the ends toward which it is directed and the appropriateness of the means to those ends. Most historians agree with Calvin Coolidge that the McNary-Haugen plan would not have been an effective means to the end it set for itself. But they all agree that the end at which the bill aimed (loosely speaking, "parity" or "equality for agriculture") was just.

From the point of view of most historians Coolidge is vulnerable on two points. First, with respect to the means, Coolidge argued that McNary-Haugen was not only unworkable but unjust. He regarded it as class legislation, a subsidy, and hence contrary to the American tradition of free enterprise. But what was the industrial tariff if not a subsidy to big business and a discriminatory burden upon

21. Ibid., p. 109.

workers and farmers? By supporting the tariff, on principle, and by vetoing McNary-Haugen, on principle, Coolidge revealed the nature of his "principles": support of big
business. Second, by vetoing McNary-Haugen, without
suggesting anything in its place, Coolidge revealed that he
was either indifferent to equality for agriculture, or intel-
lectually bankrupt, or both.

From the retrospective vantage point of most historians,
the 1920s were an historical way station on the road to the
New Deal. In agricultural thinking, as in economic thinking more generally, darkness was gradually giving way to
light. The intellectual bankruptcy of the conservatives and
the unworkable panaceas of the desperate farmers are evidence of the dark void in which the people of that age were
living. But the intellectuals, whose thinking was more
advanced, were beginning to see the shape of the future,
the so-called domestic allotment plan. Their thinking, however, was not yet an important political force ("In 1928
domestic allotment still seemed an academic proposition.")[22]
The intellectuals were not to become a political force until
the greed and folly of the conservatives had finally brought
about their overthrow. It was not until then that the daring
ideas of men like M. L. Wilson and Rexford Tugwell were
to be mated with the power of the federal government,
under the supervision of the democratic statesman, Franklin Delano Roosevelt. There is an illuminating passage in
Professor Schlesinger's *The Vital Center* in which he says
that at moments of crisis (e.g., a depression), when capitalists and workers alike are bewildered, the democratic
politician-intellectual can often outwit the logic of the class
struggle.

> Experience is a better master than any sacred myth. The
> experience of a century has shown that neither the capitalists

22. Ibid., p. 110.

nor the workers are so tough and purposeful as Marx
anticipated; that their mutual bewilderment and inertia leave
the way open for some other group to serve as the
instrument of change; that when the politician-manager-
intellectual type is intelligent and decisive, he can usually
get society to move fast enough to escape breaking up under
the weight of its own contradictions; but that, when no one
provides intellectual leadership within the frame of gradualism,
then the professional revolutionist will fill the vacuum and
establish a harder and more ruthless regime than the decadent
one he displaces.[23]

Most historians believe that the Great Depression was
such a time, and that President Roosevelt's AAA was a
reasonable alternative to the ineffectual policies of the
1920s.

The McNary-Haugen plan, simplified and abstracted from
its legislative metamorphoses, would have worked as follows. Suppose a crop such as wheat with an exportable
surplus. The price of that crop, even if it is protected by a
tariff, will sell at the world price. The McNary-Haugen
plan proposed that the government purchase, or finance
the purchase, of the exportable surplus, so as to remove it
from the domestic market. The decrease in supply to the
domestic market, which would be walled off from foreign
competition by the wheat tariff, would cause an increase in
the domestic price. The domestic price would theoretically
rise to the world price plus the amount of the tariff. The
surplus, which had been segregated from the domestic
supply, would then be sold abroad at the world price. The
loss sustained by the exporter would be made up by an
"equalization fee" imposed on all wheat farmers.

For example, suppose American wheat production in
one year to be 800,000,000 bushels, 200,000,000 of which
is the exportable surplus. If 800,000,000 bushels of wheat

23. Schlesinger, *Vital Center*, p. 155.

are bought by exporters and domestic consumers at an average price of $1.50, gross revenues will be $1.2 billion. The exporters will have paid $300 million for 200,000,000 bushels, which they can sell on the world market for, let us say, $1.00 per bushel or $200 million. Their loss of $100 million, assessed to the farmers, amounts to 12.5 cents per bushel of the entire wheat crop. (This assessment was known as the "equalization fee.") That 12.5 cents, subtracted from $1.50, gives the farmers in the end $1.375 for each bushel of their wheat, as opposed to the world price of $1.00 that they were receiving before the plan went into operation.

To summarize:

600,000,000 bushels sold at new domestic price of $1.50	$ 900,000,000
200,000,000 bushels sold at world price of $1.00	200,000,000
800,000,000 bushels	$1,100,000,000

$$1,100,000,000 \div 800,000,000 = 1.375$$

That this plan would have worked in practice as it worked on paper was believed by almost no serious person at that time and has been believed by no serious person since. The plan rested upon two assumptions, both false. The first was that higher prices would not stimulate additional production. The second was that foreign markets would remain open to our agricultural exports and would pay a price high enough to insure the success of the plan. Professor Schlesinger and President Coolidge are of one mind in thinking that the problems of additional production and retaliation from other countries would have doomed the scheme.

These problems may be illustrated with reference to the wheat crop. We confine ourselves to the example of wheat,

because the wheat farmers were the most fervent support-
ers of McNary-Haugen. Professor Koerselman, in his study
of McNary-Haugen, goes so far as to say that apart from
George Peek's explanation of how the plan would work for
wheat, "No one else ever recorded a clear explanation of
how the plan would operate when it was applied to other
commodities."[24] This reminds us of a point that we made
earlier, namely, that agriculture cannot be thought of as a
class whose members share identical interests. Quite apart
from the fact that some farmers are prosperous and some
are poor, there is the fact that agriculture is a complex and
diverse occupation. As Rexford Tugwell said in an article
published in 1928:

> Another difficulty, which seems very real indeed, is that the
> program, as it came to be framed in legislation, appealed
> only to a limited number of farmers themselves: those whose
> products go heavily into export—mostly cotton, wheat, and
> tobacco growers. A farmer in the East or Middle West, with a
> rounded mixed farming routine, can see little gain from a
> plan which depends for its success upon the manipulation of
> exports. Many farm products have an almost wholly domestic
> sale. Consequently, dairying, fruit-growing, vegetable-gardening,
> stock-raising, or even corn or hog-producing farmers are not
> enthusiastic believers in McNary-Haugenism.[25]

Leaving these caveats to one side, we take up the discussion of the wheat export situation in the 1920s. At the turn
of the century America had produced 29 percent of the
world's wheat crop. In 1900 the United States exported 200
million bushels of wheat. As the century wore on America's
exports of wheat fell. In 1913 they were only 120 million
bushels, and had averaged only 116 million bushels per

24. Gary Koerselman, "Herbert Hoover and the Farm Crisis of the Twenties"
(Ph.D. dissertation, Northern Illinois University, 1971), p. 350.
25. Tugwell, "Reflections," pp. 482-483.

year from 1900 until the war. World War I, because of its
devastating effect on European agriculture, was a boon to
American wheat farmers. Average yearly exports doubled,
to 237 million bushels, in the period 1914 to 1920. In 1920
itself fully half of America's net wheat production was
exported.

In the two decades following the first world war, countries such as France, Argentina, Canada, and Australia
expanded their wheat production. Canada alone, which
had produced a mere 56 million bushels in 1900, by the
1920s was producing 400 million bushels a year, or half as
much as the United States. By the mid-thirties, European
wheat production was 20 percent above its *prewar* average
(1909-1913), let alone its wartime average. Under the circumstances, American wheat production declined from 29
percent of the world's total in 1900 to 23 percent in the
twenties and 20 percent in the late thirties.[26]

Increased world production of wheat, of course, lessened
the demand for American wheat in world markets. But
Europe also erected tariffs to protect its own farmers from
American exports, now that the war was over and American wheat was no longer so desperately needed. France
began increasing its wheat tariff in 1926, Italy in 1928, and
Germany in 1929-30. Moreover, European governments
were taking other steps to promote domestic wheat production or to discourage foreign imports. England was
paying its farmers a bounty, France was buying part of the
domestic crop, and Italy imposed milling quotas.[27]

Writing in 1932, Bernhard Ostrolenk was sceptical concerning agricultural exporting schemes, whether for wheat
or other commodities.

26. Harold Barger and Hans Landsberg, *American Agriculture* (New York:
    National Bureau of Economic Research, 1942), pp. 52-55.
27. M. L. Wilson, *Farm Relief and the Domestic Allotment Plan* (Minneapolis:
    University of Minnesota Press, 1933), pp. 11-15.

> . . . this faith in the existence of a European market, with or
> without a form of subsidy, is not shared by the dispassionate
> searcher into recent trends . . .

> . . . the available data point to a vanishing European market
> for all grains including wheat, a diminishing market for pork, a
> satiated market for cotton, a moderate market for fruit and a
> non existent market for beef or butter.[28]

Apart from the closing of foreign markets, the McNary-
Haugen plan faced an obstacle that it could never sur-
mount or circumvent. That obstacle was the law of supply
and demand. A higher price for a given crop will tend to
increase the supply of that crop while decreasing demand
for it. This will tend to drive down the price of the crop and
offset the initial benefits from the higher price. Innumera-
ble examples of this offsetting process were adduced during the debates over McNary-Haugen, and its truth has
been universally conceded since. This flaw in the plan led
to the production controls imposed under the AAA.

Because they are so generally conceded, we do not wish
to devote additional space to the defects of McNary-
Haugen. They justify President Coolidge's rejection of the
measure. They do not, however, save Coolidge from the
charge of inconsistency. That he could denounce McNary-
Haugen as not only unworkable but unjust, while advocating
the protective tariff, is on its face evidence of Coolidge's
hypocrisy, in the eyes of most historians. Nearly all of his
academic detractors state the charge of inconsistency flatly,
as though it were as obvious as the noonday sun.

In our own thinking the truth of the inconsistency charge
is less obvious than it is apparently to most other students
of the Coolidge era. In fact, our opinion is to theirs as night
is to day: We believe that Coolidge can easily be exoner-

---

28. Bernhard Ostrolenk, *Surplus Farmer* (New York: Harper & Bros., 1932),
    pp. 62-63.

ated from the charge but that his critics find themselves in serious danger of self-contradiction when challenged to extend the principles of McNary-Haugen to occupations other than farming. This is in no way to endorse the tariff acts of 1922 and 1930. We have the gravest doubts as to the wisdom of the Republican protectionist doctrine. But the workability of the tariff is not the issue at this point. What is at issue is whether President Coolidge was inconsistent in promoting the tariff while denouncing McNary-Haugen.

We will take up the charge of inconsistency in two parts. The first is the cruder version, as expressed by Gilbert Fite in his informative book on the McNary-Haugen debate.

> To Republicans, such as Coolidge and Hoover, who were still worshipping at the shrine of William McKinley, the McNary-Haugen bill represented a dangerous change in the traditional relationship between economics and government. Hoover felt so strongly on this point that he was almost blinded to reason . . .
>
> Coolidge was bound by what Tugwell called "a stubborn determination to do nothing." There were sound economic arguments against the measure which he might have expanded, but his real opposition stemmed from a doctrinaire unwillingness to depart from laissez-faire for American agriculture."[29]

If it was true that Coolidge and Hoover opposed McNary-Haugen on the grounds that it was inconsistent with the principles of laissez-faire, then they were, of course, guilty of a contradiction in supporting the tariff. But no historian, in asserting that Hoover and Coolidge advocated laissez-faire, has ever quoted either of those men actually affirming such a belief. Historians only quote each other to prove the point. The reason is that neither man ever uttered

29. Fite, *Peek*, pp. 194, 196.

a word in favor of laissez-faire. It is certainly true that many professions of faith in the free enterprise system can be found in the speeches and writings of both men. But the same can also be said of Franklin Roosevelt. A true advocate of laissez-faire capitalism is someone like Professor Murray Rothbard, who is a bitter critic of Coolidge and Hoover both.

Liberals like President Franklin Roosevelt commonly understand themselves to be in possession of the middle ground between revolutionary socialism and laissez-faire capitalism. Conservatives like President Coolidge commonly understand themselves to be in possession of the very same ground. Each identifies the other with one of the extremes. This is nothing new in American politics. In the eyes of their opponents the Hamiltonians were monarchists; the Jeffersonians were mobocrats; Lincoln was an abolitionist; Douglas was pro-slavery. Is it not among the duties of an historian, as he sifts the political debates of the past, to discard the chaff of partisan exaggeration? What will we say of those historians who continue to parrot the charge of laissez-faire against Hoover and Coolidge, even though the charge is directly contradicted by what they said and what they did? Fortunately that charge is disappearing from historical literature as more and more historians attempt to achieve a more sophisticated understanding of the years preceding the New Deal. We summarize this brief discussion of the cruder version of the inconsistency charge by repeating two points: (1) Presidents Coolidge and Hoover are not on record as advocating laissez-faire capitalism; and (2) they pursued many policies that were incompatible with such advocacy.

The more standard charge against President Coolidge's veto of McNary-Haugen has to do not with ideology but with interest. Historians routinely assert that Calvin Coolidge was the willing servant of the business interests and hence was only interested in legislation (e.g., the tariff) designed to help business. For a typical statement of this argument we offer an extended passage from *Republican Ascendancy* by John Hicks.

> However it might be phrased, the McNary-Haugen bill as Coolidge saw it, asked government to do what government had no right to do. It called for price fixing, for an improper delegation of the taxing power, and for the creation of a vast and cumbersome bureaucracy. It was economically unsound, for the higher prices it contemplated would lead to greater overproduction and larger surpluses, while the disposal of American goods abroad at cut-rate figures would arouse foreign resentment and promote retaliation. The government, Coolidge thought, might legitimately help the farmers to help themselves. It might properly lend money to co-operatives and encourage the curtailment of production. But beyond this it should not go. The President, like his Secretary of the Treasury and his Secretary of Commerce, was in reality a devoted partisan of industry. He saw nothing wrong with a protective tariff—a tax designed specifically to help industry—but he found everything wrong with the equalization fee—a tax designed to fit the need of agriculture. No doubt he was opposed on principle, as were most industrialists, to do anything that would raise the prices of the raw materials industry had to buy, or that would raise the price of labor by increasing the cost of living. Coolidge prosperity was merely another name for industrial prosperity, and whatever might imperil that prosperity was wrong.[30]

We note first that Hicks, with respect to the economic soundness of McNary-Haugen, concedes Coolidge's main argument. ("It seems likely that Coolidge was right in objecting to the McNary-Haugen bill on economic

---

30. John Hicks, *Republican Ascendancy* (New York: Harper & Row, 1960), pp. 199-200.

grounds.")[31] In strict logic, of course, this concession presents Coolidge's critics with a difficulty. For how is his alleged partiality toward industry apparent from his veto of legislation which he (and most experts) believed would *not* help farmers and his support of legislation which he believed *would* help business? Hicks faces a similar logical difficulty at the end of the passage quoted above, when he says that Coolidge was "*No doubt* . . . opposed on principle . . . to doing anything that would raise the prices of the raw materials industry had to buy . . ." This would have been a good time to quote from Coolidge's veto messages or to cite the relevant passages. Instead, Hicks has only a single footnote for the entire paragraph that we quoted, and that footnote refers us to only a single source: Gilbert Fite. Here is Fite's commentary on the raw materials issue:

> Actually, Coolidge did not stress his most *fundamental objection* to the measure in either of his veto messages. He was basically opposed to raising the cost of living and the price of raw materials because of the adverse effect this would have on the competitive position of American industry.[32] (Italics mine.)

Now insofar as this is meant to prove Coolidge's partiality it is backward. Logically, it is necessary already to know that Coolidge is partial in order to know that he deemphasized his most "fundamental objection." He cannot be convicted by what he did not say. This reminds us of the story we once heard about the hearing preceding the internment of the Japanese Americans in World War II. The prosecutor presented his case, saying that the Japanese Americans ought to be interned for the safety of the country in time of war. The defense objected: "But you have

31. Ibid.
32. Fite, *Peek*, p. 196.

offered no evidence of any illegal or treasonous acts." To which the prosecution retorted, "Of course not, but that just proves what clever little devils they are!" No doubt the wording of Coolidge's vetoes proves what a clever little devil he was.

Professor Hicks is now down to his last argument, which is that Coolidge "saw nothing wrong with a protective tariff—a tax designed specifically to help industry—but he found everything wrong with the equalization fee—a tax designed to fit the needs of agriculture." Before we comment on the most obvious point, we should note that the equalization fee, unlike the tariff, could in no way be construed as a general revenue device. It was not intended to generate revenue for the treasury. Second, it did represent at the least a questionable delegation of the taxing power. It is by no means certain that the equalization fee would not have been struck down by the courts, as was the processing tax under the AAA.

The more obvious point is the false characterization of the tariff as "a tax designed specifically to help industry." We have already seen that the Republican administrations were eager to extend the tariff to agricultural products. We have also seen that the duty free list was constructed with the farmers in mind. Hicks himself admits that the Emergency Agricultural Tariff "placed nearly prohibitive charges on twenty-eight agricultural items"; though he contends that they were "notably ineffective in raising farm prices."[33] But John Black, dean of American agricultural economists in the twenties and a severe critic of Coolidge, was somewhat more generous.

> Tariff duties are already effective on sugar, wool, flax, lemons, oranges, raisins, and nuts. They are effective locally, or on certain grades, or part of the time, on wheat, corn, oats, rice,

33. Hicks, *Ascendancy*, p. 54.

dairy products, eggs, tobacco, potatoes, and a considerable
list of other products.[34]

Mr. Hicks treats the agricultural tariffs cavalierly, and he
may be correct in his view that they did not much help the
farmers. But this was not the view of the farmers themselves. As late as the campaign of 1932, when Herbert
Hoover charged that Franklin Roosevelt intended to dis-
mantle the agricultural tariff, Roosevelt, alarmed, rushed
out to the Midwest to deny that he had ever contemplated
any such thing.

What is undeniable, however, is that the tariff had at
least as much of an impact upon agricultural prices as the
McNary-Haugen plan would have. In saying this we do not
refer to the likelihood of the failure of the plan to achieve
its goals, although this is a striking point of contrast between
the tariff and the McNary-Haugen scheme. What we mean
is that even if the McNary-Haugen bill had been effective,
its principal beneficiaries would have been, not all farmers,
but only the producers of wheat, tobacco, and rice. In
1926, the value of the wheat, tobacco, and rice crops, as a
percentage of the value of all crops, was less than 15
percent. The value of cattle and dairy products was 28
percent. (Cattle and butter were dropped from the Mc-
Nary-Haugen bill of 1927.) The most important crop in
1926 was cotton, which accounted for just over 22 percent
of the total value of crops sold in that year.[35] But the cotton
farmers were not in favor of the McNary-Haugen plan as
such. (By which we mean the two-tier pricing system and
the equalization fee.) The cotton farmers needed loans
from a revolving stabilization fund. *And this the Republican administrations were willing to give them and did give*

34. Black, "McNary-Haugen," p. 415.
35. National Industrial Conference Board, *Agricultural Problems in the
    United States* (New York, 1926), p. 15.

them in 1929, when Hoover's farm program passed the Congress. The South finally voted for McNary-Haugen, which it had long opposed in principle, as part of a deal whereby the cotton farmers would get their stabilization fund and the wheat farmers would get McNary-Haugen.

There is no denying that the agricultural depression during the administration of President Wilson was severe; there is no denying that it continued into the administrations of his successors; there is no denying that although many farmers prospered and although farmers generally made substantial gains in the twenties, their progress never completely satisfied anybody. It is not true, however, that the Republican administrations of the twenties were indifferent to the plight of the farm. The truth is that they did everything that they could think of, within the limits of what they regarded as permissible and politically possible, to help the farmer. And the only proposed farm legislation about which they have been criticized (1) probably would not have worked and (2) was for the benefit of a minority of the farmers in any event.

We have mentioned the tariff. We alluded to President Hoover's farm program. We now repeat some observations that we made in a footnote at the beginning of chapter 3. In the early twenties agriculture was exempted from the antitrust laws. Agriculture was the only industry allowed to issue tax-free bonds. Many loan and credit programs were offered to farmers. Every effort was made to make Muscle Shoals a production site for cheap fertilizer of Southern farmers. Internal improvements—specifically with respect to inland waterways—went forward as a means of reducing transportation costs. Federal taxes were substantially reduced, and state and local governments were urged to reduce their tax burden on the farmer. The budget for the Department of Agriculture was five times that of Commerce.

But President Coolidge would not support McNary-Haugen, because he regarded it as a dangerous precedent in a free society. And in this matter, we believe, it is not Coolidge who is guilty of self-contradiction, but rather those historians who sit in judgment upon him. Mr. Coolidge was willing to extend tariff protection to agriculture as well as to other industries. But we believe that his critics, who are willing to support McNary-Haugen in principle if not in practice, would not agree to extend its principles to other industries.

President Coolidge favored a protective tariff and immigration laws as ways of promoting the prosperity of our own people and producers. Beyond that, however, he did not generally favor an appeal to the government from the verdict of the American marketplace. Accordingly, from 1921 on, nearly twenty thousand businesses each year failed in the United States. On average, for every four businesses that made money three reported losses each year.

President Coolidge was willing to provide tariff protection for agriculture as well as for industry. How could he consistently have withheld the mechanism established by McNary-Haugen from other businesses in distress? As the President said in his first veto of McNary-Haugen (1927):

> . . . but, far more important than this, I do not believe that upon serious consideration the farmers of America would tolerate the precedent of a body of men chosen solely by one industry who, acting in the name of the Government, shall arrange for contracts which determine prices, secure the buying and selling of commodities, the levying of taxes on that industry, and pay losses on foreign dumping of any surplus. There is no reason why other industries—copper, coal, lumber, textiles, and others—in every occasional difficulty should not receive the same treatment by the Government. Such action would establish bureaucracy on such a scale as to dominate not only the economic life but the moral, social, and political future of our people.[36]

36. U.S., Congress, Senate, 69th Cong., 2d sess., 25 February 1927, *Congressional Record*, p. 4773.

During the 1920s the number of automobile companies declined from 108 to 44. Many unprofitable producers of cars, like many unprofitable producers of wheat, were driven from business. Is it the position of those historians who have ridiculed and denounced Coolidge that the government would have been justified in intervening in the automobile market? Imagine how they would have screamed had Coolidge proposed that the Government lend money to exporters to buy cars off of the domestic market, so as to raise the price, and then dump those cars abroad. During the farm debates Congressman Fort raised the question whether the government ought to be willing to purchase, or finance the purchase, of automobiles if General Motors should triple its production. We believe that no historian would sanction such a scheme. Quite apart from the economic folly of the idea, it would have, *in principle*, the most far-reaching consequences for our economic and political instititions.

Conservatives in general, and Presidents Hoover and Coolidge in particular, have always been accused by their academic critics of ideological rigidity. The charge against them is that they wildly exaggerated the consequences of what in reality were minor steps toward a greater measure of federal involvement in the affairs of the country. Mc-Nary-Haugen and Muscle Shoals received stinging vetoes from Coolidge and Hoover respectively. We have, we believe, shown why President Coolidge's fears about the consequences of McNary-Haugen had some plausibility. We do not intend, however, to absolve either president from all such charges. In some instances perhaps they were too hesitant to let the government assume additional powers. On the whole, however, we are inclined to regard such charges as caricature, which caricature obscures a fundamental issue in American politics. That issue is whether there should be a presumption in favor of limited government, with respect to economic problems, or whether there should not.

Professor Schlesinger. in discussing Herbert Hoover's attempts to wrestle with the Great Depression, depicts Hoover as a man in the grip of an ideological obsession.

> In the end, Hoover, dragged despairingly along by events, decided that wherever he finally dug in constituted the limits of the permissible. Doctrinaire by temperament, he tended to make every difference in degree a difference in kind and to transform questions of tactics into questions of principles.
>
> As his term wore on, the ideological obsession grew. *He had himself done unprecedented things to show the potentialities of national action;* but anyone who went a step beyond transgressed the invisible line and menaced the American way of life. His was the tragedy of a man of high ideals whose intelligence froze into inflexibility and whose dedication was smitten by self—righteousness.[37] (Italics mine.)

We do not now wish to defend Hoover's depression measures. We believe that Professor Schlesinger makes valid criticisms of some of those measures. But it is necessary to point out that Hoover rightly suspected that there were many intellectuals (men like Professor Schlesinger) who looked upon his emergency and experimental measures as baby steps on the road to the thorough transformation of the American way of life.

Professor Schlesinger, writing a decade and a half after the first inauguration of President Roosevelt, had the following to say about the New Deal, which, of course, was itself a considerable advance beyond the depression program of Herbert Hoover: "There seems no inherent obstacle to the gradual advance of socialism in the United States through a series of New Deals." And later:

37. Schlesinger, *Crisis*, pp. 246-247.

Serious intellectual direction may give our politics a cogency
and a firmness which will maintain the equilibrium of forces
and avert the war with Russia. If we can avoid this war, if
we can contain the counter-revolution of the USSR within
clearly marked limits, we have a good chance to test the
possibilities of a peaceful transition into a not undemocratic
socialism.[38]

It goes without saying that Professor Schlesinger is no
doctrinaire socialist. He is far too pragmatic, and too committed to a view of the world as pluralistic and ever-
changing, ever to chain himself irrevocably to any narrowly
conceived economic system. And yet he is, we believe,
dedicated to the view that politics at its best is a blend of
daring and power, under democratic supervision. This view
permeates the moving peroration to the second volume of
The Age of Roosevelt:

Nothing could daunt him [Roosevelt], very little surprised
him, he was receptive to everything, and not in a passive
sense either, he received, not to accumulate, but to act; the
future which he perceived was (this he deeply believed) to
be in part his own creation. Wells summed him up: "The most
effective transmitting instrument possible for the coming of
the new world order. He is eminently reasonable and
fundamentally implacable. He demonstrates that
comprehensive new ideas can be taken up, tried out
and made operative in general affairs without rigidity
or dogma. He is continuously revolutionary in the new
way without ever provoking a stark revolutionary crisis."

38. Arthur M. Schlesinger, Jr., "The Perspective Now," *Partisan Review*,
May-June 1947, pp. 231, 242, 238. An additional quotation from the
article: "So long as Churchill lived in Downing Street, Moscow knew that
Britain offered no competition in the struggle for Europe. But the victory
of the Labor Party in the summer of 1945 brought new hope to all the
people of Europe. . . . When the Communists do succeed in finally
absorbing or destroying the Socialists, they will have virtually attained
their objective of destroying the center and reducing the alternatives to
the red and the black. The crime of the USSR against the world is its
determination to make experiments in libertarian socialism impossible."

If Calvin Coolidge is taken to be a symbol of American conservatism, and as such is rejected out of hand as an ideologue and a tool of Wall Street, then the dialogue between conservatism and liberalism, or moderation and daring, or prudence and pragmatism, is ended before it can begin. History then becomes not a source of insight and illumination, but a weapon, which we use to repel any challenges to our own smug convictions.

It is easy to convince ourselves that those with whom we disagree are not as wise or as public spirited as we are, and it may be true. But the first duty of the historian is to understand the men of the past as they understood themselves, before attempting to understand them differently or better. In this way if we err we do so after having done our best to be fair. And in the meantime there is a chance that we may learn something, which there is certainly not if we regard the writing of history as simply another forum for the expression of our own most deeply held political beliefs.

39. Arthur M. Schlesinger, Jr., *The Coming of the New Deal* (Boston: Houghton Mifflin Company, 1959), p. 588.

Four

The Mellon-Coolidge Tax Cuts

In the early 1960s, when President Kennedy proposed his tax cuts for business, and for taxpayers in all brackets, he was widely applauded by liberal economists and intellectuals. They applauded him for his pragmatism, for his refusal to be bound by the old economic myths, and for his determination to be guided not by theories but by practical results.

There was dissent. John Kenneth Galbraith denounced the tax proposals as a throwback to the days of McKinley. To be more precise Mr. Galbraith should have said that they were a throwback to the days of Andrew Mellon and Calvin Coolidge. The *New Republic* (March 23, 1963) chided the Republican scepticism toward Mr. Kennedy's tax proposals in an article entitled "Andrew Mellon on Tax Cuts."

> "I can't get it through my head," said the President of International Harvester in Chicago the other day, "how you can get more money by cutting revenue." The gentleman should read up on some recent Republican history. Actually, President Kennedy has pre-empted the Republicans on a policy which historically has more to do with GOP conservatism and "sound business principles" in government than with the New Deal or the Democratic Party.[1]

1. Donald F. Swanson, "Andrew Mellon on Tax Cuts," *New Republic*, March 23, 1963, p. 22.

The *New Republic* went on to show that despite three tax cuts during the administration of Calvin Coolidge, tax revenues increased. If it is true that the Republicans had forgotten their own past, it is no less true that the *New Republic* had forgotten its past as well, as one can see by re-reading a whole series of articles from the *New Republic* in the twenties attacking the tax policies of Andrew Mellon!

Both Mr. Coolidge and Mr. Kennedy proposed tax cuts for all, including businessmen and the rich. One main difference between them was that Mr. Kennedy cut normal tax rates while Mr. Coolidge cut emergency wartime rates, which most people believed were no longer appropriate in peacetime. Whereas the corporate tax rate was reduced during the 1960s, it was for the most part unchanged during the 1920s. The same was true of the capital gains rate.

Nevertheless, Mr. Kennedy was praised and Mr. Coolidge excoriated by most progressives and liberals. In the 1920s ad hominem attacks against Mr. Coolidge's Secretary of the Treasury were a prominent feature of the debate over tax policy; these were missing from the debate in the early sixties.

In this chapter we intend to review the tax cuts proposed by President Coolidge, as seen through the eyes of historians. Historians have typically attacked the Mellon-Coolidge reductions on two grounds, first, that they were unjust because they were intended to benefit the rich, the few, at the expense of the rest of the country, and second, that they were unsound because they contributed to the speculation and the maldistribution of wealth that caused the Great Depression. We shall take up first the question of the justice of the tax cuts and later consider their soundness.

Professor Arthur Schlesinger has devoted a chapter in *The Crisis of the Old Order* to "The Economics of Republicanism." As usual, we do not apologize for our extensive quotation:

"The Government is just a business," said Mellon, "and can and should be run on business principles." The first necessity, accordingly, was to balance the budget, and the second to pay off the debt. But Mellon's greater interest, it soon developed, was *somewhat inconsistently* in the reduction of tax rates, especially in the highest brackets. Existing surtax rates, he felt, were intolerable. A man with an income of $1,000,000 had to pay an income tax of nearly $300,000. The consequences, he declared, were already visible on every side; everyone knew "of businesses which have not been started, and of new projects which have been abandoned, all for one reason—high surtaxes." There was a difference, he warned, between taxation and confiscation; and, to restore that difference, he proposed to establish a maximum surtax rate of 25 per cent. No one, however much money he made, should be required to pay more than one quarter of his income in surtax; otherwise it would be the end of American initiative.

A tax bill which concentrated on cutting taxes for millionaires could not command unreserved enthusiasm, even in the nineteen twenties. John Nance Garner, the wily congressman from Texas, licked Mellon's tax proposals in 1924 and forced Coolidge to sign a somewhat stiffer bill. But Mellon, ever tenacious, kept chipping away each year at rates in the upper brackets. His opponents remained notably lacking in sympathy. "Mr. Mellon himself," as George W. Norris of Nebraska observed of the Mellon bill of 1925, "gets a larger personal reduction than the aggregate of practically all the taxpayers in the state of Nebraska." But such insinuations could not daunt Mellon's crusade.[2] (Italics mine.)

Let us go back to the beginning. We have a President and a Secretary of the Treasury who are of one mind. Both preach economy, a balanced budget, and lowering of tax rates. The President sets the tone:

2. Schlesinger, *Crisis*, p. 62.

With rigid economy, vigorous salvage operations and adequate
revenues from taxation, a surplus of current receipts over
current expenditures can be realized and should be applied to
the floating debt. All branches of the Government should
cooperate to see that this programme is realized.

*I cannot overemphasize the necessity of economy in
government appropriations and expenditures* and the
avoidance by the Congress of practices which take money
from the Treasury by indefinite or revolving fund
appropriations.[3] (Italics mine.)

The Secretary of the Treasury sends to Congress the
concrete recommendations:

    1. The abolition of the excess profits tax . . .
    2. The reduction of surtaxes to approximately 25 per
    cent . . .
    3. The abolition of the nuisance taxes.
    4. The necessity of having a final determination of a
taxpayer's liability and the settlement of tax claims.[4]

Moreover, the President and the Secretary turn a hard
face against the granting of a bonus. (In the words of
historian John Hicks: ". . . the Republican stalwarts in
Congress, by holding the line against the 'Bonus,' won the
undying gratitude of the business community.")[5]

Here then we have the "economics of Republicanism."
But the economics of Republicanism have attracted some
strange adherents. The above quotations are not, as one
might expect, from President Coolidge and Secretary Mellon. They are from President Wilson and his Secretary of
the Treasury, David Houston!

"The Congress might well consider," said President Wilson in his seventh annual message to Congress,

3. Woodrow Wilson, *The Messages and Papers of Woodrow Wilson*, 2 vols.
   (New York: Review of Reviews Corporation, 1924), 2:1217.
4. David Houston, *Eight Years with Wilson's Cabinet* (New York: Double-
   day, Page and Company, 1926), p. 101.
5. Hicks, *Ascendancy*, p. 52.

whether the higher rates of income and profits taxes can in
peacetimes be effectively productive of revenue, and
whether they may not, on the contrary, be destructive of
business activity and productive of waste and inefficiency.
There is a point at which in peace times high rates of income
and profits taxes discourage energy, remove the incentive to
new enterprise, encourage extravagant expenditures and
produce industrial stagnation with consequent unemployment
and other attendant evils.[6]

The Wilson Administration, like the Kennedy Administration, eschewed ideology in favor of common sense. "It
seems idle to speculate," said Secretary Houston,

in the abstract as to whether or not a progressive income-tax
schedule rising to rates in excess of 70 per cent is justifiable.
We are confronted with a condition, not a theory. The fact is
that such rates cannot be successfully collected. . . . Whatever
one may believe, therefore, about the abstract propriety of
projecting income-tax rates to a point above 70 per cent, when
the taxpayers affected are subject also to State and local
taxation, the fact remains that to retain such rates in the tax
law is to cling to a shadow while relinquishing the
substance.[7]

A man might read for some time through the works of
contemporary historians before coming across these quotations, or any hint of their existence.

Before going on to a discussion of the fairness of the tax
cuts, we must pause to correct an error in Professor
Schlesinger's account of Mellon's views. "Existing surtax
rates, he felt, were intolerable. A man with an income of
$1,000,000 had to pay an income tax of nearly $300,000."[8]

The $300,000 tax was *not*—Mr. Schlesinger to the con-
trary notwithstanding—the tax due under the "existing

6. Wilson, *The Messages and Papers of Woodrow Wilson*, 2:1140.
7. Quoted in Andrew Mellon, *Taxation: The People's Business* (New York:
The Macmillan Company, 1924).
8. Schlesinger, *Crisis*, p. 62.

surtax rates." It was the tax a millionaire would have paid under *Mellon's* proposal. Mellon:

> As an example of how the surtax operates, a man with an income of $1,000,000 has the same aggregate income as 200 men each with incomes of $5,000, but the 200 small incomes pay a tax of $38.25 each or an aggregate tax of $7,650, whereas the millionaire *under the Treasury's recommendations* will pay a tax of $298,792.[9] (Italics mine.)

The existing tax on an income of $1,000,000—and the figure Mr. Schlesinger should have used but did not—was $550,576.[10] ("Our scholarship today is more rigorous . . .") But let us not quibble over a mere quarter of a million dollars.

We turn now to the question whether it is fair to characterize the Coolidge—Mellon tax bill as one "which concentrated on cutting taxes for millionaires . . ." What Mr. Schlesinger does *not* mention, as we have had occasion to see, is often as important as what he does mention. In the present case he does not mention that Coolidge and Mellon proposed in 1924 a reduction of the normal tax rates by 25 percent for *all* taxpayers, rich and poor. It was for this reason, among others, that the tax bill was widely supported among all categories of taxpayers and in all sections of the country. But again, the popularity of the bill is not deemed worthy of mention by our historian.

A married man with two dependent children and an income of under $3,200 owed *no* federal taxes in 1924. (The equivalent of $3,200 nowadays is around $16,000.) Under the Coolidge-Mellon proposal, the tax for a similar family making twice the income ($6,000 or $30,000 in today's money) would have been reduced to $72 a year! Moreover,

9. Mellon, p. 69.
10. Ibid., p. 197.

and here is another fact not mentioned by Schlesinger, the surtax did not apply to incomes under $6,000 a year. It was not possible to cut surtaxes on such incomes because *they paid no surtaxes to begin with*. But Coolidge and Mellon did propose to raise the minimum income subject to the surtax to $10,000. And the surtax, although the maximum was to be lowered, was to remain progressive: 1 percent on incomes of $10,000 rising to 25 percent on incomes over $100,000.

Given a "tax bill which concentrated on cutting taxes for millionaires," we would naturally suppose that the chief beneficiaries of the bill would be the aforementioned millionaires. Under the Coolidge-Mellon tax cut proposal, however, 70 percent of the lost revenues would have gone to taxpayers with incomes under $10,000. The percentage that would have gone to taxpayers with incomes over $100,000 was 2.5![11] It is a matter of the greatest regret that Professor Schlesinger's readers were not presented with these figures, because they then could have decided for themselves whether or not his interpretation of the facts was reasonable. This is especially regrettable in light of the fact that the *only* statistic that he did give, as we have shown, was incorrect. We feel compelled to state our own opinion at this point, that so far as the 1924 tax cut debate is concerned, the student of the period could get a better sense or feel for the arguments by browsing through old issues of the *Literary Digest* than he could by reading prize winning history.

In his book, *Republican Ascendancy*, written for The New American Nation Series, Professor John Hicks follows Mr. Schlesinger's lead:

> The reduction of taxation for the rich and the transfer of as much of the burden as possible to the *middle* and lower

11. Ibid., p. 56.

incomes was *a matter of principle* with Mellon, and not merely of self-interest. [12] (Italics mine.)

We wish we could say that Professor Hicks wrote that line because he had confined his reading solely to Mr. Schlesinger's book. Unfortunately, we cannot. In a footnote to the paragraph in which this sentence appears we find this citation: "Andrew E. Mellon, *Taxation: The People's Business* (New York, 1924), pp. 93-94." We turn to page 94 of Mellon's book, where we find Mellon writing that existing tax rates

> penalize principally the *middle* incomes, while permitting wealth to escape by investing in tax-exempt securities and by other available methods. . . . We have under the high surtaxes a system that increases the actual tax burden on the men of *moderate incomes* and allows many of the largest incomes to escape taxation. (Italics mine.)

Andrew Mellon may have been a hypocrite, but this is not the argument advanced by Professor Hicks. Hicks argues that Mellon *in principle* favored placing more of the tax burden on the middle and lower incomes. The above statement from Mellon gives the lie to the professor's astonishing assertion, as do other statements from Mellon.

> In making its recommendations, the Treasury has been guided by the necessity first, of providing a sufficient income for the government; second, of lightening the tax burden, so far as possible, on those *least able to bear it* . . . [13] (Italics mine.)

Professor Hicks asserts that Mellon believed in a reduction of taxation for the rich and a "transfer" of the tax

12. Hicks, *Ascendancy,* p. 53.
13. Andrew Mellon, "The Business of Taxation," *The Forum,* March 1924, p. 344.

burden to the middle and lower incomes. We have seen that the bulk of the reduction in 1924 was intended for those of modest incomes, but even if this were not the case Professor Hicks's statement would be false. The reason is that tax reduction was made possible by a surplus; hence there could have been no "transfer" of the burden. It was not as if the burden was taken off of one man's back and put on to another's: the burden was taken off and cast aside.

Speaking before a Lincoln Day audience in 1924, President Coolidge delivered one of the best reasoned speeches ever delivered by an American president on the subject of taxation. As we have seen, Professor Hicks contends that Secretary Mellon wished to transfer the burden of taxation from the rich to the middle class and the poor. In his Lincoln Day address Coolidge explicitly endorsed the contrary view. Perhaps it goes without saying that the following passage in Coolidge's speech did not find its way into Hicks's book, nor did any mention of the speech, nor did any hint of Coolidge's true opinions. Nor did any of these things grace the pages of Mr. Schlesinger's book.

> I agree perfectly with those who wish to relieve the small taxpayer by getting the largest possible contribution from the people with large incomes. But if the rates on large incomes are so high that they disappear, the small taxpayer will be left to bear the entire burden. If, on the other hand, the rates are placed where they will produce the most revenue from large incomes, then the small taxpayer will be relieved.[14]

Mr. Coolidge's reasoning has hardly been mentioned, let alone challenged, by subsequent historians. ". . . in taxation, like everything else," said Coolidge,

> it is necessary to test a theory by practical results. The first object of taxation is to secure revenue. When the taxation of

14. Mellon, *Taxation*, p. 221.

large incomes is approached with that in view, the problem is to find a rate which will produce the largest returns. Experience does not show that the higher rate produces the larger revenue. Experience is all in the other way.

When the surtax rate on incomes of $300,000 and over was but 10 per cent, the revenue was about the same as when it was at 65 per cent. There is no escaping the fact that when the taxation of large incomes is excessive, they tend to disappear. In 1916 there were 206 incomes of $1,000,000 or more. Then the high tax rate went into effect. The next year there were only 141, and in 1918 but 67. In 1919 the number declined to 65. In 1920 it fell to 33, and in 1921 it was further reduced to 21. I am not making any argument with the man who believes that 55 per cent ought to be taken away from the man with $1,000,000 income, or 68 per cent from a $5,000,000 income; but when it is considered that in the effort to get these amounts we are rapidly approaching the point of getting nothing at all, it is necessary to look for a more practical method.[15]

Under the high surtaxes that were in effect until Congress reduced them in the twenties, people making very large incomes (over $300,000 a year) paid a decreasing percentage of the total surtaxes paid by all citizens.

Year	Total Surtax	Surtax on Incomes over $300,000	Percentage of Total Surtax Paid by Incomes Over $300,000
1916	$121,946,136	$81,404,194	66.8
1917	433,345,732	201,937,975	46.5
1918	651,289,027	220,218,131	33.8
1919	801,525,303	243,601,410	30.4
1920	596,803,767	134,709,112	22.6
1921	411,327,684	$84,797,344	20.6[16]

15. Ibid., pp. 220-221.
16. Ibid., p. 193.

In 1922, with the surtax at 50 percent, those making over $300,000 a year paid $77,000,000 in federal taxes. By 1927, when the surtax had been reduced to only 20 percent, this same group paid $230,000,000.[17] While the rich were paying more taxes, as Mellon and Coolidge had predicted, the working people and the poor were paying less. Speaking of the Revenue Act of 1926, David Koskoff said: "With a practical tax exemption on every household's first $4,000 of income, there was no income tax at all for most Americans."[18]

We wish to mention one more fact before we allow Professor Schlesinger to break fresh ground. We have seen that the professor hoped to leave his reader with the impression that the Mellon tax bills were intended to benefit primarily the rich. Of course, Schlesinger did not reveal any of the statistics that appear in the last few pages. In fact, as we have seen, the one statistic that he did reveal was incorrect. But it cannot be denied that Professor Schlesinger has a gift for striking images, even if he is a little weak on the facts. Accordingly, he clinches his presentation by quoting Senator Norris on the 1925 tax proposals: "Mr. Mellon himself gets a larger personal reduction than the aggregate of practically all the taxpayers in the state of Nebraska." Senator Norris did not point out that the federal tax on Nebraska's net income was less than 2 percent. Nor did he balance his statement by noting that in 1924 Andrew Mellon *paid* more federal taxes than all the people of Nebraska put together.[19] We expect a certain amount of partisanship from a politician in the heat of battle. What should we expect from a historian writing a generation after the event?

17. David E. Koskoff, *The Mellons* (New York: Thomas Y. Crowell Company, 1978), p. 237.
18. Ibid.
19. Ibid., p. 238; U.S., Department of the Treasury, *Statistics of Income from Return of Net Income for 1924*, p. 238.

We have seen that Professor Schlesinger began his discussion, or non-discussion, of Mellon's tax policies with a
mistatement of Mellon's views, and he ends by quoting the
ad hominem attack on Mellon by Norris. He now continues
for a full page to insinuate that Mellon's integrity was
questionable.

> Nor was tax reduction Mellon's only resource. What he
> could not reduce, he could often refund—a process which
> had the advantage of taking place behind closed doors. Not
> until Garner forced the revelation of the figures in 1930 did
> the country know what Mellon had done. In his first eight
> years at the Treasury, the Secretary dispensed $3.5 billion in
> the shape of cash refunds, credits, and abatements. The size of
> these disbursements mounted steadily during the period,
> except in 1927 and 1930, when congressional grumbling forced
> the Treasury to hold back. Several million dollars went to
> Mellon's own companies; other millions, as Garner took
> pleasure in pointing out, went where they promised to do
> the most good to the Republican party. Thus each of the
> seventeen individuals contributing $10,000 to the Republican
> campaign in 1930 had been beneficiaries of Mr. Mellon's
> official generosity.[20]

This paragraph is a deeply disturbing indictment of Andrew Mellon. That a man appointed to a position of high
national trust and honor should abuse that trust and that
honor by dispensing millions of dollars of public funds to
his own companies and to contributors to his own political
party, behind closed doors, is shocking. It is a total viola-
tion of the canons of public service. Our initial reaction,
upon first reading this paragraph, was to reject Mr. Schlesinger's subsequent remarks as gross understatement. ("The
Mellon tax program had—at least in the minds of skeptical
observers—its contradictions in equity and ethics.")[21]
  In the indictment as Professor Schlesinger sketches it,

20. Schlesinger, *Crisis*, pp. 62-63.
21. Ibid., p. 63.

Secretary Mellon is answerable to three charges, viz., (1) that during his "crusade" to reduce taxes on the rich, what he could not reduce he refunded *behind closed doors;* (2) that he benefitted personally by dispensing millions to his own companies; and (3) that he disbursed Treasury funds for political advantage: millions went "where they promised to do the most good to the Republican party."

The reader, scandalized, naturally inquires as to the evidence for these damning allegations, which, of course, in the text are merely asserted not documented. Not that the reader has any doubts that the documentation will be more than sufficient. The author, after all, is a respected prize winning historian, who would no doubt lean over backward to avoid staining, perhaps ineradicably, the reputation of a man who can no longer speak in his own defense. It is in cases like the present one that the best historians are most scrupulous and judicious. What then is the evidence against Andrew Mellon?

There is a single footnote for the entire indictment. The footnote refers the reader to two speeches in the House of Representatives by John Nance Garner, and to nothing else.

Congressman Garner was the leader of the Democrats in the House. He was a witty and colorful figure, who excelled in harrassing and ambushing and sniping at the Republican enemy during those sporadic guerilla actions that always accompany the main force political battles between the two parties. Normally these skirmishes are spirited, but the spiritedness contains a large measure of—as they say in Parliament—"synthetic indignation." Charge provokes countercharge, reproach meets contempt, shafts of wit are answered by vollies of sarcasm. Occasionally, of course, these partisan skirmishes turn very ugly. Such was the case during the vicious and vindictive prosecution of Senator Couzens during the Coolidge Administration or the vicious and vindictive prosecution of Andrew Mellon by the Roosevelt Administration. Such is the nature of partisanship.

But Professor Schlesinger is not a partisan, he is a historian. He is writing decades after the events he narrates. Yet in sullying the reputation of the Republican Secretary of the Treasury, he speaks only with the voice of the Democratic leader of the House! And more: On each of the two occasions when Garner attacked Mellon, Congressman Hawley, Chairman of the Joint Congressional Committee on Internal Revenue Taxation, answered Garner's charges point by point on the floor of the House. But Mr. Schlesinger's readers only see Andrew Mellon brought before the bar of history and condemned. They witness no defense of Mellon. They hear no debate. They see no citation of Hawley's speeches in our historian's footnotes.

But just because Garner was a partisan does not make him wrong. What is to be said of the substance of the charges against Andrew Mellon?

> Nor was tax reduction Mellon's only resource. What he could not reduce, he could often *refund*—a process which had the advantage of taking place *behind closed doors*. Not until Garner forced the revelation of the figures *in 1930* did the country know what Mellon had done. (Italics mine.)

If a person will go to the *New York Times* for March 4, 1924, and look on page 3, column 1, he will find the following:

> Refunds on tax payments totalling $123,992,820.94, were made by the Treasury in the fiscal year ending June 30, 1923, according to a report sent to the Ways and Means Committee by the Department.

This is one of the yearly refund figures whose revelation Garner alledgedly "forced" in 1930. Not only will the reader find in the pages of the *Times* the gross amount of the refunds, but he will also find something that cannot be found in Garner's speeches: the *names* of all companies and persons who received large refunds and the *amounts* they received. The fact is that the Treasury every year sent the figures to Congress, because every penny of refunds paid out of the Treasury required a congressional appropriation. The reader who believes that Mellon made the refunds behind closed doors might well read that part of Garner's speech where he criticizes the administration of the Joint Congressional Committee on Internal Revenue Taxation:

GARNER: . . . But I say this: That under the domination of the Republican organization in this House that chairman has not functioned as I thought he would and as I think he ought to function. He never called the joint committee together to consider these matters, except the three cases heretofore referred to.

Mr. HAWLEY: But the refunds are sent up before they are allowed.

Mr. GARNER: They certainly are. As a matter of law they are compelled to come there.

Mr. RAMSEYER: And there is an expert named Parker who does go over all of these refunds of $75,000 or more.

Mr. GARNER: That is correct.

Mr. RAMSEYER: And does he not report to the individual members of that joint committee?

Mr. GARNER: No.

Mr. RAMSEYER: But they are available to the members of that committee.

Mr. GARNER: Oh, yes, they are available to everybody here.

A MEMBER: Oh, no.

Mr. GARNER: Oh, yes. There is not a man in this body who can not walk into that joint committee and see what there is there.

Mr. RAMSEYER: It is the duty of the members of the joint committee to watch those refunds of over $75,000.[22]

To summarize: The refunds were public knowledge. The gross amounts were public knowledge. The individual amounts were public knowledge. There was, in addition, a Board of Tax Appeals established in the Revenue Act of 1924. It was independent of the Treasury. Its hearings were public. If the amount of tax at issue was over $10,000, a written record of the Board's hearing was required. That record was public.

It is true, of course, that income tax returns were confidential then, as they are now. No man could go in and peek at his neighbor's return. (Although even confidentiality was suspended for two years during the 1920s!) But this had been the case since 1917, and was not new with Mellon's administration of the Treasury.

"In his first eight years at the Treasury, the Secretary dispensed $3.5 billion in the shape of cash refunds, credits, and abatements." By using phrases such as "what Mellon had done" and "the Secretary dispensed," Mr. Schlesinger encourages the reader in the belief that the refunds, credits, and abatements were a policy devised and executed by Mellon. But this is misleading. Every year in the 1920s, tens of thousands of taxpayers received refunds, just as we do today. This is not a matter of policy set down by the Secretary of the Treasury, but simply a matter of law. But the Treasury in the twenties faced an abnormal problem, in

22. U.S., Congress, House, 71st Congress, 3d sess., 16 December 1930, *Congressional Record*, p. 874.

addition to the yearly refunds. It had to work through an immense backlog of tax returns from the war years. The income tax went into effect during World War I. The war called forth a host of complicated and confusing taxes: luxury taxes, nuisance taxes, excess profits taxes, surtaxes, etc. The Treasury was suddenly faced with the difficulty not only of administering the new income tax, but many other taxes as well, and in stupendous amounts. It was overwhelmed. Given the double circumstance of novelty and emergency, it is not to be supposed that all taxes were assessed and collected with no errors and with no differences of opinion arising between the government and the taxpayers. On the contrary, there was an enormous administrative snafu, which took more than ten years to untangle. That work fell primarily upon Mr. Mellon's Treasury Department. A large portion of the $3.5 billion dollars to which Mr. Schlesinger refers was in connection with tax adjustments and claims for the war years.

It goes without saying that in complicated tax cases there are many opportunities for differences of interpretation, even between men of integrity and good will. The Internal Revenue Service does have some leeway in assessing taxes, but it is subject to appeals to the federal courts. It would not be correct, however, to think that its leeway extended to all $3.5 billion of the refunds, credits, and abatements. For example, we have noted that in 1923 refunds amounted to $123,992,820.94.

> The large refunds in several cases resulted from Supreme Court decisions. One decision held that estate taxes paid were deductible from the gross receipts while the Internal Revenue Commissioner had ruled that this was not deductible. Another decision on stock dividends, which made them non-taxable, resulted in an aggregate refund of $70,000,000.[23]

23. *New York Times*, March 4, 1923.

In that year one court decision accounted for more than half of the refunds. Here was a case where "Mellon" was fighting to *decrease* the refunds sharply, but was defeated in court.

Congressman Hawley stated that of the refunds 28 percent were the result of court decisions and 57 percent were the result of bookkeeping or clerical error.[24] The chief staffer of the Joint Congressional Committee on Internal Revenue Taxation, Herbert Parker, in reporting on the work of the Division of Investigation, said: "The refunds and credits made by the commissioner are in general plainly correct and not open to serious criticism. A difference of opinion exists in relatively few cases."[25]

The remaining cases were controversial. But one can hardly issue a blanket condemnation even of these cases. To be just one is obliged to look into the particulars of each settlement. Professor Schlesinger has not done so. Three and one-half billion dollars is a great sum of money. Much of this sum, as we have seen, was determined in the courts or was otherwise utterly uncontroversial. Of the balance not all can be held against Mellon, even in the worst case. In the worst case all that could be held against Mellon would be the *difference* between the balance and whatever assessment his critics decided upon. For instance, Representative Garner believed that the government had been too generous to U.S. Steel. In this case, which took literally years to study (which study filled an entire room with documents), Garner believed that Steel should pay several million more in taxes than the several hundred million of its final assessment for the war years. He may have been right. The congressional committee thought otherwise. The Treasury believed that it had reached a reasonable settle-

24. U.S., Congress, House, 71st Congress, 3d sess., 19 December 1930, *Congressional Record*, p. 1133.
25. *The National Income Tax Magazine*, August 2, 1929, p. 318.

ment with Steel. If it had challenged the settlement in court, and lost, the defeat might have required it to refund substantially more to U.S. Steel. (In fact, the IRS in the twenties lost half of its court cases.) The point is that even with respect to the one case in seven that was controversial, only a fraction of the refunds, credits, or abatements allowed would have been controversial.

We believe that the tone and tenor of Mr. Schlesinger's "history" of the Mellon treasury could not have been maintained if he had made some mention of the above considerations. But there is one simple fact, suppressed by Mr. Schlesinger, which absolutely ruins his caricature of Mellon as a man bent on dispensing billions from the treasury. Common sense prompts the question that leads us down the trail of discovery to this little fact: The total of government refunds, credits, and abatements over eight years was $3,450,434,392. Is it plausible that *all* of the adjustments were made in favor of the taxpayers, as over against the government? Or does it not stand to reason that in the course of readjustment there were *additional assessments* levied against some taxpayers? The answer is that Mellon, during the eight years he "dispensed" $3,450,434,392, assessed the taxpayers an additional $5,345,202,277.[26]

"The size of these disbursements mounted steadily during the period, except in 1927 and 1930, when congressional grumbling forced the Treasury to hold back." (1) Until now we have not contradicted the impression that during the 1920s billions were pouring out of the Treasury. But this is yet another false impression. Credits and abatements were not "disbursements." No money left the Treasury. The amount of actual *refunds* was a mere $1,254,317,890. (2) The disbursements did *not* mount steadily. They were higher on average during the earlier and middle years. In

26. *Congressional Record,* 16 December 1930, p. 875.

1928, for example, they were *lower* than in 1927.[27] (3) In August of 1929 Mr. Parker said that the peak of the war backlog had passed. The figures of 1930 subsequently confirmed his prediction. The lower figure for 1930 had nothing to do with "congressional grumbling."[28]

"Several million dollars went to Mellon's own companies; other millions, as Garner took pleasure in pointing out, went where they promised to do the most good to the Republican party." By now these facts appear in a different light. Mellon's companies surely were entitled to refunds every bit as much as Mellon himself was or any other taxpayer. Mellon himself, of course, did not personally decide upon the amount of his personal refund or those of his companies. These cases, like other similar ones, went through several field audits and several Washington audits, conducted by a civil service force composed of Democrats and Republicans alike. Did they all conspire further to enrich Andrew Mellon?

". . . each of the seventeen individuals contributing $10,000 to the Republican campaign in 1930 had been beneficiaries of Mr. Mellon's official generosity." This is an especially cheap shot. Even John Nance Garner admitted he had no proof that these contributors had in any way been treated deferentially or otherwise than in strict conformity with the law. Perhaps Mr. Schlesinger in his historical research has at one time or another come across the names of Herbert Lehman, Irene du Pont, John Davis, Bernard Baruch, John J. Raskob. If so, he will recognize them as contributors to the Democratic party. They were also—as common sense might have told him—"beneficiaries of Mr. Mellon's official generosity," just as their Republican counterparts were. Can anyone suppose that this fact was not known to a prize winning historian?

27. Ibid.
28. *The National Income Tax Magazine,* August 30, 1930, p. 303.

Professor Schlesinger might well have said, if he wished to question Mr. Mellon's administration of the Treasury, that there was in a small minority of cases a gray area in the tax laws which allowed officials of the Treasury some discretion in the assessment of tax liabilities. He might then have pointed out that some congressmen and senators believed that the Treasury, in exercising its discretion, had been altogether too lenient in granting refunds, credits, and abatements to some applicants (e.g., the Mellon companies). He might then, if he wished to ascertain the truth or falsity of that belief, have investigated carefully several cases in detail. But Schlesinger did none of these things. Instead, he offered up to his readers a partisan account, from which he concealed fact after fact after fact. And what is worse, he compounded his concealment of certain facts with misstatement of others. For instance, he said that the refunds took place behind closed doors. This was no more true then than it is now. For instance, he said that the country did not know what Mellon had done until Garner forced the revelation of the figures in 1930. This is false. For instance, he said that the Treasury "disbursed" $3.5 billion. This is false. For instance, he said that the refunds "mounted steadily." This is false.

All of this is pursuant to Mr. Schlesinger's attempt to interpret the 1920s in a certain light. He wishes at every point to show that the common good had been forgotten in the stampede to make money, and that the rich were trampling the poor underfoot. If he can picture Andrew Mellon cutting taxes on the rich and secretly funneling money out of the Treasury into the pockets of the wealthy, then his purpose is achieved. Then we see an America riven by class conflict, ruled by the wealthy, and ripe for the impending crisis of the old order. It is to that crisis that we now turn.

Five

Coolidge Prosperity and the Great Depression: Was There a Cause and Effect Relationship?

It is the opinion of many historians that the Great Depression was caused by the unjust policies of President Coolidge. Professor Hicks says that in the twenties people "handed over the nation to business leadership, the Presidency along with the rest. But business leadership led straight to the Panic of 1929 . . ."[1] Nevins and Commager say that "concentration of wealth and power in many great corporations produced a national economy fundamentally unhealthy."[2] Leuchtenburg says that the Coolidge "administration took the narrow interests of business groups to be the national interest, and the result was catastrophe."[3] Schlesinger says that the administration "seeing all problems from the viewpoint of business, . . . had mistaken the class interest for the national interest. The result was both class and national disaster."[4]

1. Hicks, *Ascendancy*, p. 279.
2. Nevins and Commager, *Pocket History*, p. 406.
3. William Leuchtenburg, *The Perils of Prosperity* (Chicago: University of Chicago Press, 1958), p. 246.
4. Schlesinger, *Crisis*, p. 160.

Broadly speaking all of the above historians, along with a great many others, are adherents of what we shall call the underconsumptionist thesis. We shall allow Professor Schlesinger to state the thesis in his own words.

> Management's disposition to maintain prices meant that workers and farmers were denied the benefits of increases in their own productivity. The consequence was the relative decline of mass purchasing power. As goods flowed out of the expanding capital plant in ever greater quantities, there was proportionately less and less cash in the hands of buyers to carry the goods off the market. The pattern of income distribution, in short, was incapable of long maintaining prosperity.[5]

Too much money was going into savings and profits and not enough into wages and spending. Thus,

> The sucking off into profits and dividends of the gains of technology meant the tendency to use excess money for speculation, transforming the Stock Exchange from a securities market into a gaming-house. (By the middle twenties, the whole economic process began to focus on a single point—the ticker-tape machine with its endless chatter of stock market quotations. The torrent of excess money, pouring into the market, swept stock prices ever upward.)[6]

Professor Schlesinger, while emphasizing the purchasing power argument, also credits the Federal Reserve with pursuing, to a degree, an easy money policy that fueled the "speculative boom." (". . . the easy money policy had the effect of accelerating the inflation in the United States. And in 1928, an election year, it was impossible to get a firm decision to check the upward spiral.")[7]

5. Ibid., pp. 159-160.
6. Ibid., pp. 68, 160.
7. Ibid., p. 69.

We intend to review the underconsumptionist thesis in some detail. But first we wish to introduce into the historical record some evidence that tends to correct or moderate the impression that many people have of the nineteen twenties as a stampede to make money, and as an orgy of speculation, easy money, and inflation. In their massive study, *A Monetary History of the United States, 1867-1960*, Friedman and Schwartz characterize the twenties as a period of economic stability.

> The economic collapse from 1929 to 1933 has produced much misunderstanding of the twenties. The widespread belief that what goes up must come down and hence also that what comes down must do so because it earlier went up, plus the dramatic stock market boom, have led many to suppose that the United States experienced severe inflation before 1929 and the Federal Reserve System served as an engine of it. Nothing could be further from the truth. By 1923, wholesale prices had recovered only a sixth of their 1920-21 decline. From then until 1929, they fell on the average of 1 percent per year. The cyclical expansion from 1927 to 1929 is one of the very few in our record during which prices were a shade lower at the three months centered on the peak than at the three months centered on the initial trough. The stock of money, too, failed to rise and even fell slightly during most of the expansion—a phenomenon not matched in any prior or subsequent cyclical expansion. Far from being an inflationary decade, the twenties were the reverse. And the Reserve System, far from being an engine of inflation, very likely kept the money stock from rising as much as it would have if gold movements had been allowed to exert their full influence.[8]

Lester Chandler (*American Monetary Policy 1928-1941*) supplies much evidence to support this view.

1. "Price levels of goods and services were virtually

8. Milton Friedman and Anna Schwartz, *A Monetary History of the United States* (Princeton: Princeton University Press, 1963), p. 298.

stable after 1923." The GNP deflator was 100.0 in 1923 and 99.5 in 1929.

2. The money supply grew at an average annual rate, compounded, of 2.4 percent from June 1923 to June 1929. "One who believes that the money supply . . . should grow proportionally with the nation's productive capacity would argue that monetary policy was not too liberal but too restrictive, especially after 1927."

3. Interest rates were historically high in the twenties.

4. After reviewing earnings and dividends and prices, Chandler says, "At what stage in the rise of stock prices did they become 'unreasonably' high . . .?' Though no one can answer with confidence, I would put the date no earlier than mid-1928 and probably later."[9]

The decade of the twenties was a time of stability and great prosperity, at least at first glance. But how deep did the stability and prosperity go? Was there, beneath the surface, a widening split between rich and poor, presaging the economic earthquake to come? Professor Schlesinger presents some empirical evidence for this thesis on pages 65 to 68 of *The Crisis of the Old Order*. We will consider first the relationship between the Great Depression and the Mellon-Coolidge tax cuts.

Historians assert that the tax cuts of the twenties "made the maldistribution of income and oversaving by the rich still more serious."[10] They also say that taxes were cut on the "theory that this would stimulate business," but "unhappily it also stimulated the speculative craze of the late twenties."[11] Professor Schlesinger echoes both of these statements.

9. Lester Chandler, *American Monetary Policy 1928-1941* (New York: Harper and Row, 1971), pp. 18-29.
10. Leuchtenburg, *Perils,* p. 246.
11. Nevins and Commager, *Pocket History,* p. 406.

> . . . the Mellon penchant for tax reduction served to make
> more money available for speculation. "A decrease of taxes," as
> Mellon said, "causes an inspiration to trade and commerce."
> *With this* he injected a few more billions into a boom which
> hardly needed to be further inspired.[12] (Italics mine.)

This is one of those many passages in Schlesinger's book
that at first reading seem so plausible, and indeed telling,
but which upon analysis are revealed to be based upon
nothing more than the historian's imagination. Consider:

1. The words with which Mellon "injected" billions into
the "boom" were written in 1924. Does anyone, even
leaving aside the evidence presented above from Chandler, believe that 1924 was a "boom" year?

2. The entire tax cut in 1924, even after it had been
enlarged by the compromise with the Garner forces,
amounted to roughly one-third of a billion dollars, far less
than the "few more billions" in Mr. Schlesinger's account.

3. The corporate tax rate, of course, was *increased* in
1924. Therefore, all of the speculative money injected into
the boom must have come from other tax changes. But we
have seen, in our discussion of the tax bill, that 70 percent
of the tax reduction would have gone to people with incomes
under $10,000. Under the actual bill as it was finally passed
that percentage was larger. Of the remainder, perhaps a
tenth of a billion dollars, it is hardly likely that anywhere
near all went into the so-called boom. In short, Mr.
Schlesinger has started out with "a few more billions" and
has ended up with a small fraction of one billion.

4. In retrospect, we wonder whether the professor would
be quite so willing to label tax cuts as boom money and if so
whether he would be willing to say of John F. Kennedy
what he said of Andrew Mellon? (". . . the Kennedy pen-

---

12. Schlesinger, *Crisis*, p. 63.

chant for tax reduction served to make more money available for speculation.")

We shall come soon to the question whether corporate profits were disproportionately high in the twenties and hence whether the stock prices responding to those profits were speculative. For the moment, however, we wish to see whether the tax cuts made the maldistribution of wealth more serious. Again we quote Mr. Schlesinger:

> The Mellon tax policy, placing its emphasis on relief for millionaires rather than for consumers, made the maldistribution of income and oversaving even worse. By 1929, the 2.3 per cent of the population with incomes over $10,000 were responsible for two-thirds of the 15 billion dollars of savings. The 60,000 families in the nation with the highest incomes saved almost as much as the bottom 25 million. The mass of the population simply lacked the increase in purchasing power to enable them to absorb the increase in goods.[13]

There is a certain shock value in a statement such as this, which reminds us in a striking way that a few people are much richer than the rest of us. Again, however, when the statement is subjected to analysis, it becomes extremely doubtful whether the conclusion of the statement follows from the facts contained therein. In theory it is questionable whether the maldistribution of wealth, as such, is among the causes of the business cycle. Neither Professor Schlesinger nor any other historian, or economist for that matter, has to our knowledge shown that there is any consistent relationship between changes in the distribution of wealth and fluctuations in national income. The structure of wealth tends to change very gradually, whereas the business cycle tends to peak every few years. Moreover, we know of no consistent relationship between the magni-

13. Ibid., p. 67.

tude of changes in the distribution of wealth and the magnitude of economic fluctuations. If a nation as a whole has a
high rate of saving, i.e., chooses to spend its money on
capital rather than consumer goods, this does not necessarily mean that it must in time plunge into a depression. The
examples of Germany and Japan in our own day demonstrate
that rapid and healthy economic growth is not incompatible with a high rate of saving. On the contrary, it may be
that the rate of growth is a function of saving.

We will set aside, however, our doubts about the theo-
retical foundation of Mr. Schlesinger's underconsumptionist
thesis. We will restrict ourselves to several empirical observations. The first is that the statistics for a single year tell us
nothing about the dynamics of a situation. In other words,
no economist, given the statistics on the distribution of
wealth in a given country at a given time, could deduce
from those figures alone whether the country was on the up
slope or the down slope of the business cycle, or whether it
was likely to prosper or languish in the future. We doubt
whether he could even extrapolate from a whole series of
such statistics covering many years the future of the economy. But Professor Schlesinger offers us the figures for
only one year and discerns in this still-life the portents of
disaster.

Although the figures are not perfectly trustworthy, it
seems to be the case that in the twenties the rich were
getting richer and the poor were getting richer, but the
poor were getting richer at a slower rate. But this process,
as we mentioned above, goes on at a snail's pace. In 1921,
the top 5 percent of the population received 25.47 percent
of the income. In 1929, the top 5 percent received 26.09
percent of the income. Can this be what toppled the world
into the Great Depression?[14]

14. *Historical Statistics of the United States* (Washington, D.C.: U.S.
Department of Commerce, 1975), p. 302.

However that may be, it certainly cannot be true that the worsening of the maldistribution of wealth was due to Mellon's policy of relief for millionaires. The information that we have already introduced concerning the tax bills has shown that they cannot be properly called tax bills for millionaires. In 1923, people making less than $10,000 carried 20 percent of the federal income tax burden. By 1929, their share of that burden had shrunk to 2 percent! If corporate profits taxes are included we find that people making less than $10,000 accounted for less than 1 percent of federal income tax revenues in 1929. In absolute terms the decrease in the burden on such taxpayers is even more apparent. During a period when the aggregate income of people making less than $10,000 was rising, their income tax payments fell, from over $130 million in 1923 to less than $20 million in 1929. It is only a tiny exaggeration to say that Coolidge and Mellon completely removed the burden of federal income taxation from the backs of poor and working people between the time Coolidge entered the presidency and the time he left. Meanwhile, the very small fraction of the population that made over $10,000 per year was being taxed more heavily, both absolutely and as a percentage of the whole tax burden. In six years the aggregate taxes paid by tax payers in this group increased 87 percent; by 1929 they were paying virtually all of the personal income tax being received by the government.[15]

We have seen that the distribution of income changed very little in the nineteen twenties. This fact is consistent with the well-known fact that the distribution of income is remarkably stable over long periods of time. We have also seen that during the twenties the tax burden progressively shifted from the people of low and moderate incomes to the well-to-do. What will we say then to Professor Schlesinger's

15. *Statistics of Income 1923*, p. 30; *Statistics of Income 1929*, p. 34.

final argument—to which he devotes several pages—namely, that business in the twenties was making excessive profits at the expense of workers?

We note first of all that the professor, as usual, places the whole burden of a massive thesis upon the scrawny frames of two or three facts. The thesis, briefly stated, is that the large productivity gains of the twenties went into profits rather than wages, and that this "diversion of the gains of efficiency into profits was bound to result in a falling off of the capacity of the people as a whole to buy." The sum total of the evidence for this conclusion is as follows:

> 1. The output per man-hour in industry rose about 40 per cent during the decade.
> 2. Through the decade, profits rose over 80 per cent as a whole, or twice as much as productivity; the profits of financial institutions rose a fantastic 150 per cent.
> 3. Between 1923 and 1929, output per man hour in manufacturing rose almost 32 per cent, while hourly wages rose but slightly over 8 percent.[16]

We cannot believe that anyone would allow himself to be persuaded that the twenties were a time of inordinate profits and lagging wages merely on the basis of these meager scraps of economic history. As a preface to our own discussion of the same subject, we make two points. First, the reader will get from Mr. Schlesinger no real sense of the economic gains made by labor in the twenties. (The closest he comes to hinting at it is on page 111 of *The Crisis*.) Professor Leuchtenburg, on the other hand, although he shares Mr. Schlesinger's view that wages lagged profits ("Management had siphoned off gains in productivity in high profits . . .") at least has enough of the scholar's candor to mention these gains: "essentially unchanged from 1890

16. Schlesinger, *Crisis*, pp. 67-68.

to 1918, the real earnings of workers—what their income would buy—shot up at an astonishing rate in the 1920's."[17] The second point that we wish to make is that profits are typically more volatile than wages. Therefore, the relationship between wages and profits is not constant, and profits will look very different when viewed from different time frames. For example, one can show profits rising at a fantastic rate vis a vis wages if he measures the increase from cyclical trough to cyclical peak. On the other hand, looked at from peak to trough profits do worse than wages. With these points in mind we turn to Mr. Schlesinger's facts.

When we put Schlesinger's figures side by side, we see that "through the decade" profits rose 80 percent while hourly wages rose 8 percent from 1923 to 1929. Productivity during the same time rose 32 percent. Now although Schlesinger does not say so, "through the decade"—as one discovers after backtracking through the sources—means *1922* to 1929. In 1922 the nation was just coming out of one of the worst depressions in its history. In that year profits had not yet reached 60 percent of their 1916-1920 average. So Mr. Schlesinger goes from that year to the cyclical peak in 1929 and discovers that corporate profits were rising at a fast clip. Since he subsequently uses the years 1923-1929 for the hourly wage increase, the reader might be interested in knowing the increase in profits between those years. It was 38.6 percent, rather close to the productivity increase for the same period (32 percent).[18]

But here is a curious thing: Mr. Schlesinger did not get the 80 percent figure from its original source; he got it from an essay by Paul Douglas. In that same essay, Douglas discusses the magnitude of the real wage gain for urban

17. Leuchtenburg, *Perils*, pp. 178, 245.
18. William Crum, *Corporate Earning Power* (Stanford: Stanford University Press, 1929), pp. 327-338; *Statistics of Income 1928 and 1929*.

manual workers in the twenties, but Schlesinger does not use that information. Instead, he goes to yet another source to get his 8 percent *hourly* increase. Interestingly enough, the figure given by Douglas (which tallies with the estimates made by other serious students of the wage question) is 20 percent![19] In lieu of the increases cited by our historian (profits 80 percent, wages 8 percent) we now have profits at 39 percent and wages at 20 percent. Schlesinger neglected to add to the rate increases the increases in the numbers of workers employed. This would have given him the increase in the aggregate purchasing power of the working class. (Leuchtenburg, by the way, gives the increase in corporate profits 1923-1929 as 62 percent; he does not document this figure, and it is not correct.)

We now turn to a look at profits in a longer perspective. As we do so we repeat an earlier point, namely, that we know of no study or argument that proves that "excessive" profits are the cause of the business cycle. We quoted Leuchtenburg earlier to the effect that the real earnings of workers did not rise in the three decades prior to the end of World War I. Meanwhile, profits were rising to an all-time high. In the decade following the end of the war the average annual wage per wage employee in constant dollars rose 18 percent.[20] During that same time corporate profits rose only 5 percent. The fact is that at the peak of the New Era in 1929 profits still were short of their wartime peak. Not until 1928 did profits reach even their 1916-1920 *average*. And in the meantime, of course, GNP was growing rapidly.

Let us go beyond the confines of the war and the twen-

19. Paul Douglas, "Purchasing Power of the Masses and Business Depressions," *Economic Essays in Honor of Wesley C. Mitchell* (New York: Columbia University Press, 1935), p. 120.
20. National Bureau of Economic Research, *Recent Economic Changes*, 2 vols. (New York: McGraw-Hill Co. Inc., 1929), 2:771.

ties alone, for a look at profits during the first three decades
of the twentieth century. From 1900 to 1929, corporate
profits in the United States averaged 8.2 percent of the
national income. From 1920 to 1929, they also averaged
8.2 percent. When matched against the decade 1910 to
1919, the profits of the twenties look anemic, 8.2 percent of
national income versus 9.7 percent of national income 1910
to 1919. In order to place the profits of the twenties in the
worst light, let us compare them with prewar profits (1900
to 1914). We see that in the twenties profits took a little
over 1 percent more of national income than they did in the
earlier period (8.2 percent versus 6.9 percent). At the same
time, it must be noted, compensation of employees rose by
five percentage points, from 55 percent of national income
to 60 percent of national income. This was its high for the
first three decades of the twentieth century. In short,
profits were only slightly higher vis a vis employee compensation in the nineteen twenties than they were in the
prewar period.[21]

What do all of these figures mean? Frankly, nothing. We
believe that they have little relevance to the question now
at issue, that is, what caused the Great Depression. The
truth is that in a dynamic economy the relationships between
various totals (e.g., farm income, labor income, profits,
etc.) will vary over time. Some relationships will be more
stable, others less. For example, the relative importance of
farming in the American economy has been declining practically since the beginning. On the other hand, employee
compensation as a percentage of national income has been
fairly constant in this century. There does not seem to be,
however, any cause and effect relationship between any
given set of subtotals and the business cycle.

21. *Historical Statistics*, p. 236.

Our own opinion based upon this research is that the nineteen twenties were not a time of a significant rift in the incomes of rich and poor; they were not a time when the national administration proposed a discriminatory tax policy; they were not a time when profits were growing at an extraordinarily high rate or were grossly out of line with previous experience.

These facts render Mr. Schlesinger's thesis problematic at best. There is another that renders it impossible. Let us first restate that thesis briefly. It is that as the country grew wealthier during the "boom," wealth became even more badly distributed. This had the consequence of reducing mass purchasing power. Instead of becoming mass purchasing power and clearing the market of goods, additional wealth was disproportionately saved, whence it became investment or speculation. This overinvestment created yet more goods, which could not be bought because of the failure of mass purchasing power to keep pace with production.

There is a simple empirical test of this thesis. If it is true that as income increases, a larger share than before goes into investment and a smaller share into consumption, then it follows necessarily that consumption will fall as a percentage of the total. As Mr. Schlesinger put it, "There was proportionately less and less cash in the hands of buyers." We need only look then to see whether consumption expenditures were falling as a percentage of Gross National Product in the twenties.

The figures are given in table 1.

Table 1

Total Consumption Expenditures as a Percentage of Gross National Product, 1920 to 1929

1920	67.7
1921	78.4
1922	76.7
1923	73.9
1924	77.0
1925	73.0
1926	74.2
1927	75.2
1928	75.9
1929	75.7
Average 1920-1929:	74.8
Average 1922-1929:	75.2

These figures lead Professor Temin of M.I.T. to dismiss Professor Schlesinger's thesis out of hand:

> For a recent statement of the underconsumptionist thesis, see Schlesinger . . . The concept of underconsumption has been abandoned in modern discussions of macroeconomics, although the idea that consumption was depressed before the onset of the Depression by an unfavorable distribution of income occasionally reappears. A glance at Table 1, above, however, shows that the ratio of consumption to national income was not falling in the 1920's. An underconsumptionist view of the 1920's therefore is untenable.[22]

22. Peter Temin, *Did Monetary Forces Cause the Great Depression?* (New York: W. W. Norton & Co., Inc., 1976), pp. 4, 32.

Conclusion

In the hands of a historian like Arthur Schlesinger Jr.,
history becomes a weapon. It is wielded in the fight to
advance a political cause. Perhaps that cause is a good
cause, a just and noble cause. With this use of history we
do not now intend to quarrel.

It may be instructive, however, to look at political history not from the point of view of the partisan historian but
from the point of view of the student. By the "student" we
mean the person whose mind is still agitated with the
struggle to replace his opinions about politics with knowledge about politics, a person whose thinking has not yet
crystallized into wisdom or quieted into settled opinion.

To have knowledge of something is to be able to give an
account of that thing and to defend the account against
possible objections. This implies that the knower has heard
and mastered opposing points of view, or that the learning
process involves a dialectic from which no relevant fact or
argument is excluded. The goal of partisan history, on the
other hand, is not knowledge but right opinion, not truth
(though partisan history may well be true or contain truths)
but political victory. Accordingly, in partisan histories the
student hears either no dialogue or a carefully staged dialogue. He is therefore in the position of a juryman who is
obliged to render a verdict after hearing only the prosecution's case.

What follows is a review of a few of the simple rules for
the writing of history that aspires to be judicious rather

than lawyerly. As we go through them we will give counter-examples from Mr. Schlesinger's corpus to show the difference between taking sides before a full hearing of the evidence and taking sides after such a hearing.

1. THE HISTORIAN SHOULD ATTEMPT TO UNDERSTAND THE MEN OF THE PAST AS THEY UNDERSTOOD THEMSELVES, BEFORE ATTEMPTING TO UNDERSTAND THEM DIFFERENTLY OR BETTER.

To begin with, this is a precept of simple logic. It is hardly possible to know that we have understood the men of the past better than they understood themselves, unless we first know how they understood themselves. Beyond that, this rule is an injunction against misrepresentation, especially caricature. Was Coolidge, for example, crazy about wealth? Did he exalt the morals of a peddler? Was he an advocate of laissez-faire capitalism? Or did he not rather articulate a somewhat more sophisticated set of beliefs, which—in the first instance—deserves a straightforward presentation? The partisan historian, like the politician in the heat of battle, feels free to caricature the opposition. But the serious student of politics will escape superficiality only if he thinks through the best arguments put forward by contending parties to a political controversy.

A simple example will serve to differentiate between the serious and the superficial. In *The Vital Center,* Professor Schlesinger refers to "the fantastic belief of Mr. Hoover that the federal government should not . . . feed starving people."[1] The context of this remark is a discussion in which Schlesinger shows how conservatives represent the interests of the plutocracy and justify those interests by an ideology—a set of fantastic beliefs, if you will. Hoover's fantastic belief is cited to prove his ideological rigidity and his official indifference toward the downtrodden.

1. Schlesinger, *Vital Center,* p. 28. The full quotation: "the fantastic belief of Mr. Hoover that the federal government should not build a power project at Muscle Shoals or feed starving people."

Now, of course, if Hoover actually believed that the government should let people starve before enlarging its own powers and responsibilities, then he was indeed an ideologue and a hard-hearted man to boot. But how utterly incongruous, that the man whose reputation as one of the great humanitarians of our century resulted from his feeding of starving Europeans in World War I, should refuse to feed starving Americans during the Great Depression. In truth, Hoover never subscribed to the fantastic belief that is alleged to be symbolic of his ideological rigidity. Schlesinger's assertion is belied both by Hoover's words and by his actions during the depression. Hoover, as president, authorized the release of wheat held by the government for use in the relief effort. And he was prepared to go much further if necessary. As he said on February 3, 1931:

> . . . I am willing to pledge myself that if the time should ever come that the voluntary agencies of the country together with the local and state governments are unable to find resources with which to prevent hunger and suffering in my country, I will ask the aid of every resource of the Federal government because I would no more see starvation amongst our countrymen than would any Senator or Congressman . . .[2]

This is a small example of caricature, but it has a larger significance. Franklin Roosevelt is often portrayed by Mr. Schlesinger and others as the pragmatic mean between the ideological extremes of left and right. This was also the way Roosevelt frequently portrayed himself, and it may be true. But it certainly was not Hoover's understanding of the relationship between himself and Roosevelt. Hoover understood *himself* to be in the middle of the political spectrum, between the laissez-faire capitalists on one side

2. Herbert Hoover, *Memoirs*, vol. 3: *The Great Depression 1929-1941* (New York: The MacMillan Company, 1952), p. 56.

and the social democrats and revolutionaries on the other. He may have been wrong in this. But however that may be, a historian hardly makes a contribution to a genuine understanding of the New Deal by condemning its opponents as ideologues for holding beliefs that they never, in fact, held.

2. WHEN RELATING A HISTORICAL CONTROVERSY, THE HISTORIAN SHOULD DO HIS BEST, WITHIN REASON, TO GIVE A FAIR ACCOUNT OF BOTH SIDES OF THE CONTROVERSY.

"The true obligation of impartiality," in the words of Lord Charnwood, is that the historian "should conceal no fact which, in his own mind, tells against his views." This is not an injunction against taking sides or stating an opinion after all the telling facts are out on the table. But in the writing of history, the temptations of selectivity and suppression are powerful. It is often true that the reading of a few pages in the *Congressional Record* gives a much more rounded view of a political debate than can be found in the pages of a history book. The adversary system at least insures that each side will be heard as it wishes to be heard, and that it will have the opportunity to leave no point unanswered.

On pages 236-238 of *The Crisis of the Old Order*, Professor Schlesinger has a discussion of President Hoover's Reconstruction Finance Corporation (RFC). He is critical of it on several counts, some of them persuasive. But let us take note of his methodology. The following paragraph is a perfect vignette of Schlesinger's standard operating procedure.

> For the first five months, RFC operations were kept secret—to some extent, even from the Democrats whom the RFC law required to be appointed to the board of directors. 'Several months passed,' Jesse Jones of Texas, the dominant Democrat in RFC wrote later, 'before Chairman Meyer and Secretary Mills seemed to think it necessary to regard the

> Democratic directors as their equals . . . Apparently they
> expected us blindly to do their bidding.' And, if it was bad to
> tell things to the Democratic directors, it was even worse to
> tell them to the people. In particular, Hoover objected to the
> publication of RFC loans on the ground that publicity might
> invite the very disasters—the run on the bank, for example—
> which the loans were intended to prevent. Jones, however,
> received this argument with skepticism. And the President did
> not strengthen his case by using secrecy to obscure the
> character of RFC loan policy.

Here we have the charges of secrecy and partisanship. These charges appear frequently in *The Crisis of the Old Order,* as we saw for example in Schlesinger's account of Mellon's Treasury. In the present case, the Democrats on the RFC were being treated unfairly by the Republicans, Meyer and Mills. In particular, "RFC operations were kept secret" from them.

(a) We pass over without comment the propriety of blaming the Republicans by quoting a Democrat who was a party to the partisan disputes within the RFC. We only remark the similarity between this passage and the earlier one in which Schlesinger condemns Andrew Mellon out of the mouth of John Nance Garner.

(b) Follow carefully the flow of the narrative: "And if it was bad to tell *things* to the Democratic directors, it was even worse to tell *them* to the people." (Italics mine.) What were these *things* that the Republicans were not telling to the directors and to the people? Schlesinger immediately continues: "In particular, Hoover objected to the publication of RFC loans . . ." Aha, says the reader, gliding swiftly over the flowing prose, RFC loans were kept secret from the Democratic directors and the people. Not so fast, gentle reader. RFC loans from the first moment had to be approved by the directors, including the Democratic directors. The loan operations were not, and could not, be kept secret from the directors.

(c) What then were the dark secrets withheld from the Democrats? Let us see how artfully a prize-winning historian handles quotation to achieve a desired effect.

> 'Several months passed,' Jesse Jones of Texas, the dominant Democrat in RFC wrote later, 'before Chairman Meyer and Secretary Mills seemed to think it necessary to regard the Democratic directors as their equals . . . Apparently they expected us blindly to do their bidding.'

We note first that the quotation has two parts separated by an ellipsis. The first part is taken from page 517 of a book written by Jones; the second part is taken from page 73 of the same book. The two quotations have to do with two entirely unrelated incidents. One incident had nothing whatsoever to do with secrecy. It concerned a personnel squabble. Jones was upset because, in his view, Meyer was peremptory and high-handed in the selection of staff for the RFC. Jones opposed Meyer in the first major clash over personnel, and prevailed over him.

One can squeeze just about a thimbleful of secrecy out of the second episode, in which Jones was upset not over any "RFC operations" but simply because he was not informed earlier about the deteriorating financial condition of the Central Republic Bank of Chicago in June 1932. The sequel, which Schlesinger omits, shows the insignificance of the "secrecy" charge. As the financial crisis of the Central Republic Bank developed, it was Jesse Jones who was put in charge of the RFC operation to rescue the bank! So much for secrecy.

We have seen that Schlesinger quotes the Democrat, Jones, to establish the partisanship of the Republicans, Meyer and Mills. Let us now complete the quotations from Jones, of which Schlesinger has given us fragments. Jones, page 517:

> Several months passed before Chairman Meyer and Secretary
> Mills seemed to think it necessary to regard the Democratic
> directors as their equals, a fact that brought on clashes with
> Mr. Meyer and sometimes differences with Secretary Mills.
> *When Mr. Mills could not attend our meetings, Under*
> *Secretary Arthur A. Ballantine represented the Treasury.*
> *He was most helpful. He treated us Democrats as if we had a*
> *share in the responsibility.* (Italics mine)

Jones, page 73:

> Apparently they expected us blindly to do their bidding. *I*
> *hated to see General Dawes leave our corporation. He had*
> *a broad and sympathetic appreciation of our whole economic*
> *situation.* (Italics mine)

Mr. Schlesinger, as we now see, has included just enough
of the two quotations for us to read the criticism of the two
Republicans, Meyer and Mills, but has ended the quotations just soon enough so that we are spared the praise of
the two Republicans, Ballantine and Dawes.

There is another reason why Schlesinger does not find it
appropriate to mention Jones's praise of Dawes or, for that
matter, Jones's participation in the rescue of the Central
Republic Bank (known as the "Dawes Bank" even though
Dawes was no longer a director). For on the very next
page, page 238 of *The Crisis of the Old Order,* Schlesinger
insinuates that there was something fishy and improper
about RFC assistance to the Central Republic Bank: "The
circumstances by which Dawes's bank received prompt
assistance from the agency he had just left while the unem-
ployed were denied federal aid roused natural speculation." It is hardly convenient for Schlesinger to cast the
shadow of favoritism over Dawes on one side of the page
while Dawes is basking in the sun of Jones's praise on the
other. Nor is it convenient to mention that it was not

Dawes but Jones who urged RFC support for the Central Republic Bank. Like a good lawyer, Schlesinger knows when to speak and when to hold his tongue.

(d) As Bertie Wooster might have said, there are times when one wants to hear all about Jesse Jones and then there are times when one doesn't. Consider:

> In particular, Hoover objected to the publication of RFC loans on the ground that publicity might invite the very disasters—the run on the bank, for example—which the loans were intended to prevent. *Jones, however, received this argument with skepticism.* (Italics mine)

Jones in fact did receive this argument with skepticism in his book about the RFC published in 1951. But—as Schlesinger well knows—in 1932, at the time of the debate over the Garner Amendment to publicize the loans, Jones and all of the other Democratic directors of the RFC, along with Hoover and all of the Republican directors, opposed publication.[3] Perhaps Jones had forgotten this when he wrote his book twenty years later. Faulty memory cannot be Professor Schlesinger's excuse.

(e) During the transition from the Hoover to the Roosevelt administration, Hoover implored Roosevelt to intervene with Congressional Democrats to stop publication of the lists of RFC loans. Roosevelt refused. Whether his refusal aggravated the great banking crisis of 1933, we cannot say. But shortly after Roosevelt became president, he quietly put an end to publication of the lists. One can read through a great many history books before learning this. Mr. Schlesinger does not mention it. In his own defense perhaps he would say that fire must be fought with fire. History must be used as a weapon against malefactors

---

3. James Stuart Olson, *Herbert Hoover and the Reconstruction Finance Corporation, 1931-1933* (Ames: The Iowa State University Press, 1977), p. 72.

like Herbert Hoover. Secrecy and partisanship must be fought with secrecy and partisanship. No doubt this is the best way to win political wars. It is not always the best way to understand them.

3. THE HISTORIAN SHOULD NOT PASS JUDGMENT ON THE MEN OF THE PAST ON THE BASIS OF FACTS THAT THEY DID NOT KNOW OR COULD NOT REASONABLY HAVE BEEN EXPECTED TO KNOW

In retrospect, we often see clearly what should have been done in a given situation. But the men on the spot rarely possess such clarity. This is in part why we honor as statesmen men whose vision penetrates farthest into the haze that always surrounds the present. There is no reason for honoring someone for seeing what is obvious to the meanest capacity. But history is full of surprises, which, by definition, cannot be foreseen. Just as no one deserves special honor for seeing what is plain to all, so no one deserves blame for not seeing the unforeseeable.

The following is a choice example of partisanship carried directly from political life into the history books. In the late summer of 1951, Herbert Hoover gave a speech decrying political corruption. In the course of the speech he alluded to recent scandals in the Truman administration. Professor Schlesinger, upon hearing of this speech, became feverish with moral indignation and fired off a letter to the *New York Times*. It was printed on September 12, 1951, and in it he denounced Hoover as a hypocrite because he had sat silently through the Teapot Dome scandals a generation before. Said Schlesinger, in part:

> Far from objecting to official corruption then, Mr. Hoover sat in entire complacency as Secretary of Commerce, while his colleague, the Secretary of the Interior, sought to loot the government of sums which make the deep freezers and free hotel bills of the Truman Administration vanish into insignificance . . . On March 12, 1923, eight days after Fall's hasty resignation from the Interior Department, Hoover

wrote to him: 'In my recollection that department never had
so constructive and legal a headship as you gave it.' . . .

Mr. Hoover's current appearance as a guardian of the
public morals assumes that the American people have
completely forgotten the indisputable facts of his public
record.

Two days later, Mr. Schlesinger was mortified when
Lewis Strauss wrote to the *Times* to clarify some of the
"indisputable facts" of Hoover's record. It turned out that
(a) Fall's resignation was not "hasty" but had been announced
well in advance; (b) Hoover's letter to Fall was written
months *before* the scandal broke; and (c) Fall was finally
convicted of his crimes by the Hoover administration.

Six years passed, and this exchange with Strauss faded
into a minor embarrassment on Schlesinger's public record.
In 1957, Mr. Schlesinger published *The Crisis of the Old
Order*. At the beginning of chapter eight, pages 54 and 55,
he recounts how after World War I the "high-minded
conservatives"—the "men of character"—were replaced
by the "big moneyed men." And more than that, the men
of character "cheered on the new dispensation" of big
money and thereby "contributed to their own degradation." While describing the replacement of character by
money among conservatives, Schlesinger liberally tars Henry
Cabot Lodge, Herbert Hoover, and William Howard Taft
with the brush of Teapot Dome, and once again quotes
Hoover's letter to Fall! This time, however, he has his
flanks covered:

This was written before the Fall scandals came out; but it was
addressed to a man whom Charles Evans Hughes found a
long-winded bore, and whose humbuggery seemed so patent
that William Allen White could not believe his eyes. (And,
as early as March 1922—a year before the Hoover letter—
Secretary Wallace had called attention to the transfer of the
naval oil leases.) . . .

> Thus the high-minded men contributed to their own
> degradation. Hughes, frosty and clearheaded, remained an
> exception.

Professor Schlesinger wants to have his cake and eat it too. He wants to show that the "virtuous Herbert Hoover" somehow contributed to his own degradation, even while admitting that Hoover's letter was written before the Fall scandals broke. "This was written before the Fall scandals came out; but . . ." But what? Charles Evans Hughes might have thought Fall a long-winded bore, but there is no evidence that he thought him a criminal or even a bad manager of the Interior Department. Hughes was mainly irritated by Fall because Fall trespassed onto his turf in foreign policy. Mr. Schlesinger does not tell his readers this, but in the very place where Hughes spoke of Fall as a long-winded bore, he confessed that he never suspected him of anything worse:

> He would discourse at length on foreign affairs, showing
> neither acumen, discretion, nor accurate knowledge. But he
> thought he was an authority. His flow of words without
> wisdom was very boring to me at least, and I think to
> others. I had little to do with him, *but I did not suspect him of
> anything worse than vanity and mental indigestion*. (Italics
> mine)[4]

It was, in fact, Hughes who issued a statement to the press on January 31, 1924, in which he absolved the rest of Harding's cabinet from complicity in the intrigues of Fall and his co-horts. Hughes stated that the oil leases "were never brought before the cabinet for its decision." The initial transfer of the oil leases from the Navy to the Interior early in the Harding administration, to which Schlesinger refers, is irrelevant to the alleged degradation of Hoover.

4. M.J. Pusey, *Charles Evans Hughes* (New York, 1951), p. 427.

The transfer was perfectly legal and was done with the approval of President Harding himself.

In his attempt to prove the degradation of Hoover, Schlesinger once more finds omission to be a faithful ally. On page 52 of *The Crisis of the Old Order,* barely two pages before we see Hoover degrading himself, Schlesinger tells the story about the day Harding "took Hoover aside and asked him vaguely what he should do if, say, there were scandals in the administration." Or rather we should say that Schlesinger tells half the story, for he leaves out Hoover's report of his reply, which was: If there is a scandal, "Publish it, and at least get credit for integrity on your side." It would hardly do to have Hoover uttering these words on one page if his self-degradation is to be the centerpiece of the next.

There is an interesting footnote to Schlesinger's effort to blacken Hoover's character. After completing this discussion of the degradation of the conservatives, Schlesinger goes on for the next forty pages or so to depict the New Era of Coolidge and Hoover. We have reviewed parts of this material in previous chapters. A good deal of it is ad hominem. For example, on page 63 Schlesinger mentions the Treasury employee who, upon leaving government service, "soon showed up on Mellon's personal payroll, where he turned to the Secretary's private account the knowledge accumulated in the public service."

Having waded through the sewer of the New Era, we come at last to Chapter 12 ("The Politics of Frustration"). In this chapter our eyes are lifted up to the idealism of the old Wilsonians.

> The people had made their choice, but not all the people. From the start of the decade, there had been another view of the New Era. In May 1921, Franklin K. Lane, Woodrow Wilson's Secretary of the Interior, the close friend of Franklin

D. Roosevelt, lay in his room at the Mayo Clinic,
wondering about death. 'If I had passed into that other land,
whom would I have sought—and what should I have done?'
A parade of images passed through his mind. 'For my heart's
content in that new land, I think I'd rather loaf with Lincoln
along a river bank.' His thoughts drifted to the life he was
leaving. 'Yes, we would sit down where the bank sloped
gently to the quiet stream and glance at the picture of our
people, the negroes being lynched, the miners' civil war,
labor's hold ups, employers' ruthlessness, the subordination of
humanity to industry,—His scrawl broke off. The next day
they found him dead.

The old Wilsonians watched the New Era in indignation
and contempt. They were men who had known the exaltation
of idealism. They had dared to act greatly and risk greatly.
They saw after 1920 a different America moved, as they
conceived it, by ignoble motives.

They saw, as Schlesinger had put it earlier, an America
coming to be dominated by the "big moneyed men," among
them Edward L. Doheny, oil millionaire, later to be accused
of bribing Albert Fall in the Teapot Dome scandal. On
page 49 of *The Crisis of the Old Order*, we see Doheny
looking forward to the New Era:

> On Friday, March 4, 1921, Doheny should have felt better.
> The Bolshevists were now gone from Washington; and the
> new administration was one in which men like Doheny, who
> had contributed $25,000 to its arrival, felt at home. The
> change from Woodrow Wilson to Warren Gamaliel Harding,
> from the high-minded and lofty-visioned intellectual to the
> handsome small-town sport, could not have been more
> reassuring.

Take it all in all, Schlesinger paints a touching picture of
the high-minded idealists making a gallant rear guard stand
against the onslaught of the big moneyed men. A touching
picture, or a touched up picture? It certainly helps Schle-

singer's portrait of the old Wilsonians not to mention that Doheny, who was a Democrat, had contributed $50,000 to the arrival of the Wilson administration in 1912. It also helps not to mention that Franklin K. Lane, Secretary of the Interior under Wilson and close friend of Franklin Roosevelt, believed—like his successor, Albert Fall—in the private development of government oil lands. For this belief he was bitterly attacked by conservationists. Nowhere can we find any mention of this in Schlesinger's book. In 1920, a bill was passed, which, among other things, permitted some leasing of government oil lands. A month later, Franklin K. Lane, a man who, so to speak, had known the exaltation of idealism, resigned his post and took a $50,000 a year job with the Doheny oil interests, where, as Mr. Schlesinger might have said but did not, he turned to Doheny's private account knowledge accumulated in the public service. No doubt all the while he was watching with contempt the ignoble motives of the New Era, which he was prescient enough to foresee before his death in May 1921, less than two months after Harding took office.

Some years later, when Doheny was being investigated by the Senate for bribing Albert Fall, he let it slip out that several former members of Wilson's cabinet had been on his payroll at one time or another. "I paid them for their influence . . ." said Doheny. This was a very uncharitable thing to say about a fine group of men who had known the exaltation of idealism, and no doubt it was Mr. Schlesinger's desire not to be uncharitable toward the men of the past that caused him not to mention this remark by Doheny anywhere in *The Crisis of the Old Order*.

4. THE HISTORIAN SHOULD GET HIS FACTS RIGHT.

We have it on the authority of the most eminent historical authorities that America in the 1920's was the Whore Babylon, prostituting herself for money and material things.

The idealism of the Wilson era was in the past; the
Rooseveltian passion for humanitarian reform was in the
future. The decade of the twenties was dull, bourgeois, and
ruthless. 'The business of America is business,' said
President Coolidge succinctly, and the observation was apt if
not profound. Wearied by idealism and disillusioned about
the war and its aftermath, Americans dedicated themselves
with unashamed enthusiasm to making and spending
money. Never before, not even in the McKinley era, had
American society been so materialistic, never before so
completely dominated by the ideal of the marketplace or the
techniques of machinery.[5]

The unlikely pimp for this great whore was the dour
Puritan, Calvin Coolidge. In discussions of the twenties his
name is invariably linked—as in the above quotation—
with the ethics of acquisitiveness.

Somehow the new business idealism, so much of it devoted
and sincere, had not wholly transmuted the acquisitive
impulse underneath.
   Perhaps it was the gap between principle and action: the
men who talked of character in their clubs while they plotted
to get on preferred lists and into insiders' pools; or who
spoke eloquently of service at Rotary while cursing out
farmers, workers, foreigners, and intellectuals in the locker
room . . . Despite the noble words and the lofty hope, to
many the New Era seemed at heart only a stampede to
make money . . .
   And so it seemed: the single motive had been nurtured
until it drove out all others. Joseph B. Eastman, a
distinguished Wilson appointment to the Interstate
Commerce Commission, protested in 1925 against the
prevalent philosophy. The pursuit of private gain did not seem
to him, he said, *as it evidently did to Coolidge*, "the only
impelling force in human beings" which could produce
desirable results; "indeed, I would go so far as to say that
the most important services to mankind have been the

5. Nevins and Commager, *Pocket History*, p. 410.

products of higher motives." But only a few were left to
heed such sentiments—to feel, with the old Wilsonian, Daniel
C. Roper, that the ideals of the Founding Fathers had been
forgotten.

The whole nation, Dan Roper lamented, was caught up in
the "money madness"—churches, schools, homes, everything.
Instead of trying to help their fellow men, Americans were
trying to make money out of them.[6] (Italics mine)

But what if, in fact, the pursuit of private gain did not
evidently seem to Coolidge (or to most Americans) "the
only impelling force in human beings" which could produce desirable results? In March, 1920, for example, Coolidge wrote the following critique of William Graham Sum-
ner:

> I do not think that human existence is quite so much on the
> basis of dollars and cents as he puts it. He argues in one place
> that the enunciation of great principles has had little to do
> with human development; that America became democratic
> through economic reasons rather than the reasons that came
> from the teachings of philosophy and religion. He nowhere
> enunciates the principle of service.

Many historians depict the twenties as the apogee of
business rule and influence. This apogee was reached by
way of a long struggle between the privileged and the
common run of people, a struggle that, in their view, has
been the central theme of American politics and perhaps of
politics simply. Throughout American history, according to
this interpretation, the idealism of a Roosevelt, a Wilson,
or a Roosevelt alternates with the business mentality of a
McKinley, a Taft, or a Coolidge. By the 1920s, although
the promise of political equality in the Declaration of Independence had in some measure been fulfilled, through the

6. Schlesinger, *Crisis*, pp. 74-75.

enlargement of political participation, the emancipation of the slaves, and the enfranchisement of women, less satisfactory progress had been made toward economic equality and democracy. In fact, the trend was such that the nation was steadily coming under the control of a small economic oligarchy, which posed a genuine threat to the economic, and perhaps the political, rights of the citizens.

We may say then, by way of summary, that for some historians the mainspring of American political history has been the class struggle, and 1929 was the crisis of capitalism.

It goes without saying that this is not necessarily a Marxist thesis. Most American historians, however open they may be to certain of Marx's ideas, are not votaries of Marx's entire system of thought.[7] For, even if we say nothing of the fact that the discovery of the concept of the class struggle was disclaimed by Marx, American historians obviously would view the crisis of capitalism with alarm for the fate of democratic institutions, whereas the true revolutionary would hope to see democracy swept away by the onrush of revolution. For such historians, the New Deal represented the last chance for democracy, which they, unlike the communists, supported.

But what if the New Era was not simply an intensification of the class struggle leading up to the crisis of capitalism in 1929? What if, for example, the fight over McNary-Haugen was not a class struggle between wealthy businessmen and poor farmers, but between Midwestern business and Eastern business, between Midwestern agriculture and Southern agriculture, between grain farmers and dairy farmers, between farmers and consumers?

---

7. "Marx himself, for all his abstract and polemical pronouncements of an anti-liberal character, was a man whose general flavor remains western, and whose thought can be assimilated into the democratic tradition." Schlesinger, *The Vital Center*, p. 64.

What if, for example, the tax burden was not shifted from the wealthy to the poor in the twenties but was instead removed entirely from the backs of the poor and assumed by the well-off? What then becomes of the notion that the government was simply the tool of the wealthy classes?

If it is true that the working classes improved their material living conditions more in the decade from the end of World War I to the onset of the Great Depression than in virtually any other ten year period in human history, then what becomes of the argument that Coolidge was indifferent to labor?

If the Great Depression did not result from a policy of unjust taxation, which contributed to the collapse of purchasing power—if it was instead perhaps the result of technical errors in the management of the money supply, as recent scholarship in economics has suggested—what then becomes of the crisis of capitalism?

Simply put, what if Calvin Coolidge and his political friends did not believe, did not say, and did not do much of what has been ascribed to them?

Someday someone will write a good history of the twenties. It will not be condescending. It will not be narrowly partisan. It will not pass judgment with the smug superiority of hindsight. It will be open, ample, gracious, and true. It will be written with the awareness that the transition from the New Era to the New Deal was one of only three or four critical turning points in American political history, and as such offers to the student of politics a priceless opportunity to learn about the character of the American regime. For it is at these turning points that the fundamental issues of American politics are revealed with an unusual clarity to any historian who has eyes to see. Only of the work of such an historian could we justly say that "Histories make men wise."

Index